Okay, I'll Do It Myself!

BY *BARBARA A. CURRY*

Illustrated by Don Higgins

Random House  *New York*

Okay, I'll Do It Myself!

A Handywoman's Primer That Takes the Mystique out of Home Repairs

Library of Congress Catalog Card Number: 70–140697

Manufactured in the United States of America

9 8 7 6 5

*To Soph, who weaned me on (or with?) a hammer,
and to Jean and Doze, who have picked up after
me almost ever since*

Contents

Who, Me?

To the Miss or Mrs. who has a towel rack with rickets, a faucet with sinusitis or a home anemically disposed—the prescription is: DON'T "let George do it." DO it yourself. Cringe at the thought? Then go back to your five-legged chaise and paste free-floating ostrich feathers back on your boa. This book is for those of you with Georges around somewhere (be he husband, lover, handyman, man friend or apartment superintendent) who—

1. will do the project . . . eventually;
2. use the Seabee approach. For you younger folk, this derives from World War II. In this context it means: get out every tool you own, regardless, make a big mess, swear a lot, drink oceans of beer and use a railroad spike where a two-inch nail would do;
3. use the CIA approach. This involves huge amounts of talking, thinking, checking, measuring, planning and drawing up of things. Finally, doing-day dawns . . . and the hardware store is closed.

One exception is George the engineer type. He'll keep you squared away in more ways than one. He's neat, intense, precise, careful, clean, prompt, honest and a big bore. If he's your handyman, great! If you're married to him, pity!

So there you have it. If there aren't at least three small-type projects haunting you, I'll turn in my spirit level. Carry on . . . and above all, don't panic.

B.A.C.

Musts
&
Miscellanies

or *What You Need*

and Need to Know Before

You Do It Yourself

One-Upmanship at the Hardware Store

The friendly, fusty-dusty, junk-packed hardware store, unfortunately, has just about had it. Today's version is a prepackaged nifty, gifty houseware store. If you're lucky enough to have the old kind around, get thee to it. There you can buy one of something, not six for 75¢. You can also get relevant advice and learn a bit to boot. Do your homework (read on, that is) so you can be as clear as possible with the hardware man about what you're up or down to. If the store's worth its Molly (page 17) you'll even find being somewhat helpless can help.

But beware when you brave those "other places." Being helpless will only make them help themselves, not you. Always go forth with as much authority as you can muster. If you can manage it, put together a shipshape list. One on graph paper does wonders! (Remember the paper with little blue- or green-lined squares you used to draw "let's pretend" house plans on in school?) Believe me, cutesie grocery-list paper just goads on unscrupulous types. If possible, in all cases bring a sample of the "thing" you want.

Sprinkle terminology around, but don't get carried away with the sound of your own voice. One neophyte I know had impressed a somewhat expert by casually dropping that she had used a plumb bob. Then she blew the whole bit by adding, "But I didn't know how to read it."

As one sage (me) put it: "A little knowledge is a delightful thing, since it's usually more than the other person has." Screw up your courage and use it.

Tool Up

The old saw about "a poor workman blames his tools" is just that. The truth is that a poor workman with good tools can do almost anything. A hammer has it all over the heel of a shoe.

You won't need or want all the tools listed here. (The ones with the * are the vitals.) But just knowing what they're about allows you to "tool-drop" at Ye Olde Surly Hardware Store. If you're married, I implore you: get your own bunch of tools. Even if *he* hammers his thumb better than a nail, *he* thinks of *his* tools as he does *his* razor.

Some words of caution—tools are not toys. They are meant to cut, shave, scrape, fasten and make holes in materials that are a lot tougher than skin and bone. Treat them with respect, and needless to say, keep them out of the reach of children.

Clippers, Wire. There are those that just cut wire (1) and then there is a kind (2) that cuts wire and also acts as pliers. I have both —the first I use to cut wire clothes hangers and my toenails. The second, however, is more practical for you, since it can do several jobs. The flat, fine-lined jaws are particularly good for holding or tightening little flat-sided things like nuts (see page 22). The wire-clipping middle does exactly that, whether you're wiring a lamp, decking the halls or creating a devastating centerpiece for the table.

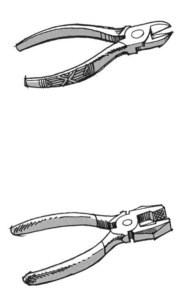

Drill, Electric. Although not asterisked, you may soon find yourself coveting this tool. If the idea sounds scary to you—remember, if you can use an electric mixer you can manage an electric drill. You can drill holes in almost anything —and fast—depending on the type of bit you use. The bit's the part that actually makes the hole. All the rest of the drill holds the bit steady, supplies the muscle and gives you something to hang on to.

A bit used for wood and sheet metal (kitchen-cabinet type) looks like ⟐══⟐⟐⟐⟐⟐⟐⟐. You can buy sets of bits increasing in diameter size from $\frac{1}{16}''$ to $\frac{1}{4}''$. Naturally, the size of the bit determines the size of the hole you drill. For plaster, you need a masonry bit.

⟐══⟐⟐⟐⟐⟐⟐

It has a carbide tip that grinds through finish plaster, rough plaster, brick and cinder block. These bits, too, are sized by diameter, but a $\frac{1}{4}''$ and/or $\frac{3}{8}''$ will do for you. Now, here's the confusing part.

The kind of drill we're talking about is called a $\frac{1}{4}''$ or $\frac{3}{8}''$ drill (there are indeed bigger drills, but they're for putting canopies in the sidewalk and signs on buildings), which has nothing to do with the size of the hole you're drilling.

The ¼″ or ⅜″ describes the non-drilling end of the bit, which you insert in the "nose" (actually the "nose" is called a chuck; I don't know why, but it is) of the drill itself. The ¼″ and ⅜″ figures indicate the maximum diameter this drill should handle. The "nose" hole can be made smaller for the smaller-sized bits. Three little teeth inside will close in and around on the bit. First, tighten by hand to get the bit centered and lightly held. Then, take the accompanying chuck key and fit it in each of the three holes that control the teeth. Keep the bit centered and tighten slightly in each hole in turn. Never do this when the drill is plugged in; you just might set off the trigger and chew up a finger. When all systems are go, you operate at right angles to what you're drilling.

Many of these drills and other portable tools come with three-pronged plugs on the cord. The third prong acts as a "ground" and guarantees a no-shock performance. If you don't have a three-holed outlet handy, you can buy a three-holed plug to go in the two-holed outlet. The hanging wire on the plug goes behind the center screw of the outlet plate. Just loosen the screw slightly and slip

the wire under it. Naturally, the screw is often painted over. Use a nail file or a hacksaw blade to remove the paint from the slot.

Drill, Hand. This drill will do most of the above, only you have to supply the muscle. To use the mixer analogy again, this is the hand-eggbeater approach. As such, it is much heavier going. You probably won't have enough brawn to do brick and cinder block; however, for beginners it is a good starter. Since high speeds are not involved here, you tighten the chuck by hand.

Flashlight. If you don't have one, for heaven's sake get one. A flashlight is indispensable for contact-lens losers, lights-out times (except those emotionally predetermined) and peering into the dark areas of drains, cupboards, etc.

The problem with flashlights—not always their fault—is their infuriating proneness to be dead or dim when you need them most. Unless you're one of those hateful people who remember to check miscellany routinely, my advice is to put a flashlight where you will see it often. Make your choice a kitchen or bedside-table drawer, in with the linens or silverware—just don't bury it. Maybe you'll remember to check the batteries before you need it, not after.

Hammer, Claw. A hammer can be used to tenderize round steak, crack black walnuts, or mash woody stems of flowers so that they won't thirst to death. For our purposes, however, the front part of the hammer drives nails into surfaces and the back part pulls them out. Don't be fooled into buying a cute little light one, even if it has a sequined "Hers" on it. A good hefty hammer does the job in half the time.

Ice Pick. Do those of you under thirty know what this is? Way back in the dark ages (my childhood) the iceman cometh for real and brought ice by the block. The ice company *gave* you an ice pick for chopping purposes. Now you have to buy them (miracles do happen—you still can); my last one cost 19¢. The ice pick is for making holes: starter holes for wood screws; extra holes on belts and sandal straps; marking holes to show you where you want to pound, screw or drill. It also pries dripped-over candle ends from their holders, and, heated, the ice pick

will make nice, round holes in plastic.

*Knife, Putty. Another inexpensive, indispensable helper. Basically, it's a thin-bladed, noncutting, flexible knife that can either lift things up (like old wallpaper) or smooth things down (like Spackle). I've never yet used mine with real putty. You'll see it referred to under projects like Moving In and Moving Out, Paint Removing, Wallpaper, and Window Opening. Although not mentioned elsewhere, cleaned up it makes a fine spatula for flattening cookie dough.

*Knife, Razor-Blade. There are two basic versions: one uses an actual razor blade, the other a special razor-type blade. The first can also be used to scrape off paint. You can do without either and grasp a single-edged blade in a sweaty hand, but it's chancey. Some foolish gals have been known to grasp a double-edged blade. I did once! 'Tis true, blood is a difficult stain to remove, especially from wallpaper. Get one; it's very cheap. With it you can safely cut through cardboard, matte board, wallpaper, vinyl wall coverings, carpet tile and foam cushioning. All this sort of activity dulls the blade at a rapid rate. When the

blade starts to drag, you'll know. Don't be chintzy. Replace the blade . . . the whole project will go easier and be neater.

Planes, Wood. These inventions make those marvelous little wood curls that Heidi (or some moppet of her ilk) loved watching Grampy for. Speaking plainly, they need real wood to work well. They won't shave a smidgen off most things you'll want to shave a smidgen off of, like plywood, plastics or hollow doors. There's not much solid wood these days, so forget a plane unless you pine to be a casket-maker.

*Pliers. Slip-jointed pliers seem to be what the experts call these (it?— like scissors, one is always plural). They are also called lobster claws, at least mine are. Anyhow, the two parts slide back and forth to adjust the jaws (mostly when you don't want them to) to hold on to, turn or pull out objects of various sizes, up to about 1¾″ in diameter. If you don't want the jaws to chew up the object you're working on (for instance, a chrome nut), put tape or a wide rubber band around it or do likewise to the jaws of the pliers. Band-Aids make good substitutes if you're out of tape.

Plumber's Helper. Grandly called a rubber force cup, this is really a big suction cup with a handle. The M.O. (*modus operandi,* or method of operation) is to set up a push-and-pull action that unclogs drains and johns (pages 83 and 90). It offers great fringe benefits for those who wash curtains or other large articles either in the bathtub or basement stationary tubs. Gently work the suction cup up and down to get an old-fashioned but effective washing-machine action. The motion pulls the suds up through the fabric to loosen the grime without a lot of heaving, hauling and hard scrubbing on your part.

Saw, Hack. This saw has tiny, close-together teeth. It's great for cutting rigid, smooth materials such as metal and plastic, like Lucite and Formica, without chipping the edges. Unless you're bent on pipe-fitting or have a yen for cutting plastic, you don't have to own one. However, it's so inexpensive and it will cut hambones. A hacksaw blade alone can come in handy (see page 55).

Saw, Hand. This is just what it says it is, something to saw by hand with. The one for you is about 2 feet long. It saws solid wood, ply-

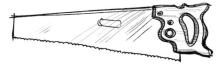

wood, hardboard, plasterboard, table legs, chair legs and sometimes fingers. A saw can be a storage problem for apartment types, but you'd be astounded how many people (males mostly) show extra interest when you casually mention between martini sips, "I have a saw."

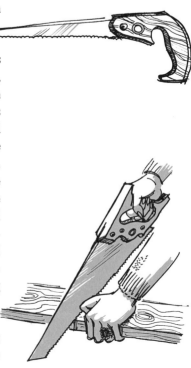

*Saw, Keyhole. This little gem is for making openings (square, round, rectangular, whatever) in things like the backs and bottoms of old chests where you've decided to put the hi-fi and have no place for the cords to go (see page 104). Purists say holes are all this little saw will do. Don't believe it! The "keyhole" will chomp through solid wood, plywood, hardboard, plasterboard, even bread. It's slower and harder going than the larger hand-saw, but unless you're plotting big projects this will do fine.

Something should be said about sawing in general. Draw a line to mark where you want to saw. To ensure a good start, put the non-saw-holding hand down and with your fingers grasp the edge of whatever you're sawing. Bend your thumb so that the first knuckle lines up the saw on the line and guides it while you saw slowly and lightly on the mark. Once you get in the groove, saw away!

Scissors, Kitchen Utility. Other than the obvious, these shears cut matchstick bamboo, thick-napped or shag rugs better than anything available. Again, they are easier to use than the usually recommended plain scissors. The latter works OK, but it's slow, slow plowing and hard on the thumb.

Scraper, Wood. This comes in various sizes and heftiness with blade widths of 1½", 3" and 4" or 5". Choose the size depending on what you're scraping. For getting paint and varnish off big areas, the broad blade makes the work go faster. The narrow blade obviously works better on smaller surfaces. You use the scraper by pulling it along the surface of wood. You can turn the blade or replace it by loosening the center screw.

Screwdrivers. Even without vodka, these come in more sizes, shapes and varieties than almost anything. Most of them are bad. Before we talk about the screwing end, let's consider the grip end. Beware of the deep-fluted plastic kind. It's a fast blister builder. If you can't find any other kind, wear an old driving glove for palm protection when using it. The hollow-ended plastic one is easy on the skin, but it will probably cave in when you take a hammer to it to pry open things like boxes and windows. (Naturally, you're not supposed to do this, but you will, and it usually works quite well.) The best screwdriver handle is made of solid, slightly fluted wood.

Now for the screwing end. It comes in two basic designs—

straight and Phillips, or star-shaped (a four-pointed star, that is— Phillips must have been an agnostic). Live it up and buy three different ones; measuring end to end, two straight, one 5" to 6" long, the other 11" to 12", one Phillips, 8" to 9".

The blades on the straight screwdriver come in different thicknesses. You'll almost always get a thin blade with the smaller screwdriver. Look for a medium thickness on the blades of the larger ones. These will screw (or un-) almost any screw in sight with the exception of set screws. These are the very small screws that allow extra towel racks to look built in (see page 91) or hold up the nut-hiding covers on legged wash basins. Unless there's a jeweler in your life, forget a special little screwdriver like he uses.

You can usually use one prong of your eyebrow tweezers and get by.

*Spirit Level. Here's a gismo to help you put up shelves and to hang wall lamps straight. All you have to do is "read" the bubble and adjust accordingly. When the bubble is centered between two lines, not off to the right or left for horizontals, or way up or down for verticals, you're in business. Spirit levels come in varying lengths and degrees of expensiveness, ranging from a cheap 3" one you can attach to a string to make it work over longer distances to the much longer professional carpenter and bricklayer models. A spirit level somewhere in the middle of this range, 10" to 12" long, should be about right for you.

Staple Gun. This gun literally shoots staples into cardboard, plywood and wood. As such, treat it with same care you would a real gun. Ten times faster and easier than tacking, it's particularly good for small upholstering jobs à la dinette seats and benches. If you decide to buy one, get a good, powerful gun. I didn't. While mine's all right for softer woods and the thinner plywood, the staples won't take on hard woods like oak or fasten wires on baseboards.

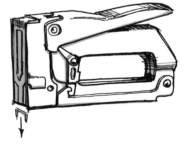

Tape, Measuring. Made of flexible metal, this tape curls up out of the way inside a case. The better versions stretch to 12 feet and have a brake which locks the tape at any point to keep it from heading for the home case. When you're doing a project *all* by yourself, it's mighty helpful.

Wrench, Adjustable Crescent. This is great for really hanging on to nuts (square or hexagonal, see page 22) to tighten or loosen them. Most of the time you can manage with pliers, but someday a project may be lurking that needs this tight-fisted approach. Invest then.

Wrench, Pipe. Not necessary unless you decide that before you're old and gray, no one will ever fix your leaky sink pipe or replace the innards of your toilet tank. This wrench is pretty hefty, but it needs to be. However, it's simple to use. Just adjust the parallel jaws until they fit snugly against whatever you want to undo or do. Check the nut size of your project before purchasing this item. Perhaps the aforementioned crescent wrench can handle it. If so, opt for that. It's more versatile.

Yardstick. Like the ice pick, this old-timer is a good friend. You can measure with it, of course, or draw lines, hold down one end of paper determined to roll up, hit the dog or fish things out from under or down from overhead. Surprisingly, some hardware stores still give these away.

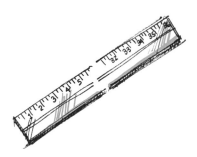

Things to Use Tools With and On

A complete list of all these goodies would match the index in Bartlett's. Be content with any or all of the following items and add to them as you become more involved and experienced. Besides beer and sneakers, finding a place to stow this stuff can be a problem. If you're determinedly organized, pacify yourself by buying a couple of clear plastic boxes with nice, neat little compartments. Being a disorganized type, it took me years to give in. Shoe boxes add a fanciful touch while holding a passel of tubes, cans, sandpaper, tape, etc. Don't toss out wide-mouthed jars or coffee cans. They're splendid for the multitudinous nails, tacks, brads, screws and the like. One of my favorite squirreling places is in the canister marked FLOUR. It's the biggest. Besides, who uses enough flour these days to command counter space? If by some quirk you do, no doubt you'll find another extra someplace marked COFFEE, TEA or SUGAR.

Beer. Depending on your capacity (if it's low, stick to the soft drinks), beer is as alcoholic in the drink line as you should go. Booze, stepladders, hammers and all sorts of things really don't mix. Reward

yourself afterward, while you're
waiting for the shelf you've put up
to fall down. When it doesn't, have
another.

Fasteners, Wall. A clumsy name but
as good as any, and that's what the
boys in the back room call them.
The term is used to cover a wide
variety of devices that hang or hold
heavy objects (like bookshelves) or
lighter ones (like paper-towel dis-
pensers) to solid or hollow walls.
There are different lengths and
diameters suited to different projects. All work pretty much on the
same idea—expansion. The most
popular and useful are discussed
here.

SHIELDS, PLUGS AND ANCHORS,
made of lead, fiber or plastic should
be used for solid walls or in thicker
hollow walls or for attaching
smaller fixtures (see page 51).
The lead version looks like
or ; the fiber ;
the plastic . All of
these fasteners expand against
the insides of a hole you've previously drilled when a screw is
screwed in (redundant but clear,
eh?), or in the case of the plastic it
can work as above but will also expand somewhat behind thinner sur-

faces such as the ubiquitous hollow door. After you've had bathroom-door hooks and racks pull out for the umpteenth time (why is it robes and wet washcloths weigh a ton?), try these.

Hollow-wall expansion bolts, made of metal, are, not surprisingly, used for hollow walls. These bolts expand *behind* the wall, not *in* it as do anchors, shields and plugs. To make it easy for yourself, ask for a Molly. This is a brand name, but everybody knows what you're talking about. There are some others, but I tell thee true, you ask for a Molly and you get a Molly. Here's

what it looks like .

A bolt comes with it. What you must know is the diameter and depth of the hole you're going to drill (the bit will tell you). See page 52 for how. With these measurements you can get the size you need without trying to crack the code of Molly sizes—it's weird. A good hardware store will translate for you. The correct size is important because the Molly has to fit firmly against the back surface of the drilled hole.

This is how it works. Drill a hole, insert the Molly, tighten the bolt with a screwdriver until you can't tighten any more. Then unscrew the bolt. The Molly "body" stays firmly in place. Pull the bolt out and use it to put up and secure whatever it is you're putting up. Here's what goes on behind the scenes, even though you can't see it happen.

P.S. (Plain Stupidity) For years I didn't know how Mollys really worked (just knew the name), so I used them to expand *in* the wall, like shields. Many a much-volumed bookshelf stayed up nicely in spite of this ignorance, but the cost is about eight times that of shields. So why blow the dough? However, if you're suddenly seized by inspiration or energy on a Sunday afternoon and you only have Mollys, it's great to know they will work this way.

Fillers. Your putty knife can swing into action here, before you paint or move, to cover up cracks or fill holes with—

ALL-PURPOSE TYPE. Although this is a relatively new product to me, from its packaging you suspect it's been serving householders for years. Called water putty, it comes in powdered form. The directions say it will, without shrinking, seal, fill and hold together everything from ceramic tile to wood. When it is dry, you can screw into, saw or nail it. So far, to the extent I've used it, this putty has lived up to its promises and, as such, could be the answer to a fixit maiden's prayer. Even with seemingly extravagant claims, this unassuming product is so cheap you won't believe it.

PLASTER TYPE. Usually called "spackling compound," you can buy this under various brand names, one of which is Spackle (generic use obviously put an end to this manufacturer's exclusivity because everybody spackles whether they're using Spackle or another of the many varieties). It comes in either

powder or paste, and in cans or tubes. The paste version is better for you because it's already mixed to the smooth, proper consistency that stays where you put it. The tube is a better buy for you unless your spackling job is considerable. You either use it all or can roll it up toothpaste fashion so it won't dry out between jobs.

WOOD TYPE. A fibrous, plastic compound that can be stained to match wood or bought in a limited range of wood colors. After it dries you can nail or screw into it just like God's original. Maybe it's me or perhaps those "expert" instructions, but I find I dodge this if I can. To me, this filler is hard to use, drying almost too fast, sticking to your fingers better than it stays in the hole (yes, I resort to them because it sticks even more to a putty knife).

Glasses, Safety. Not needed for a good many chores, but absolutely a must for any job that involves things that might splash, drip, fly, ricochet or blow in your eyes. Unless your chore involves sharp hunks, like brick or tile chips, even your own glasses or sun glasses can save you some grief. Around $2 a pair, and shatterproof at that, safety glasses are good insurance.

Gloves. I should say, a glove, right or left, depending on your sidedness. Actually, what I'm talking about is an old leather-palmed driving glove or a lined leather glove. It can save you from real blisters when you're facing a big screwing job, putting together furniture or hanging bookshelves.

For onerous tasks such as removing paint, there are bunches of clear plastic gloves. You tear them off as needed, use, then toss out. Although they look big enough for King Kong, amazingly, they cozy up to the smallest hands and are most workable (hot, though!).

Glue. Once almost totally dependent on a dead horse, the glue works of today are chemical marvels. Although there are a myriad of good sticking glues available, rarely if ever do they quite live up to their label claims in one way or another. Overall suggestion: The more porous the material—i.e., fabric or dry wood vs. glass—the less surface sticking power you get. For these cases, apply a thin layer of glue and let it dry. This coat acts as a sealer. Then apply another coat for real. Generally this system works, but never, despite ads to the contrary, expect glue to hang a trapeze. It won't. The only glue

produced (watch the fine print)
that comes close to trapeze-hang-
ing is epoxy. A relatively new dis-
covery, epoxy can be confusing because the term really is an adjective describing a process rather
than the product itself. That's why
you'll find epoxy glue, epoxy paint,
epoxy finish, and so on. What is
involved is an on-the-spot mixing
of two components, a suitable
waiting period to allow the two to
have a chemical interaction that
can produce a fantastically strong
bond. Although it sounds sexy, it
isn't—it's just epoxy.

Nails. Let's classify anything you should hit with a hammer as a
nail. (For exceptions, see Hammer, Claw, page 16.) However,
we'll subdivide and explain a little so you can sound knowing
at you-know-where. Although there are literally dozens of kinds
of nails, about all you have to start with are common nails
, finishing nails , plaster or masonry
nails , and the little ones like brads (why a
finishing nail 1½" or under becomes a brad is a man-made
mystery) and tacks

The common nail has a head that makes hitting it a whole lot
easier, but the head also shows even if you try to paint over it.
Mostly I use it to make a starter hole for screws, or on rough
work where appearance doesn't matter. The finishing nail doesn't
leave it's head sticking out and won't show at all if you take
another nail (after the first nail is in), put its point on the so-
called head of the nail in the wall and pound a couple of times,

driving it below the surface. Incidentally, there is a special tool

called a nail set for this purpose. Fill in the hole with water putty or wood filler, even Spackle, for a smooth surface.

A plaster nail is still a horseshoe nail to me. I got away with referring to it by that name until I got blank looks in New York City. Those plus the newer, less primitive versions forced a change. They hold firm, even in some (not all) of the worst plaster. I have used them at a downward angle for heavy mirrors and pictures (also see Shelves, Putting Up, page 158). They're not dainty, however, and sometimes take a chunk out of the walls. But what is Spackle for, anyway?

Brads and tacks are a bore. Brads are for when you're framing pictures, which is also a bore but cheaper than having it done for you. Tacks are hardly ever used, if you invest in a good staple gun.

Nuts and Bolts. The Puritan Ethic has made these sound so basic you probably should get some just for old times' sake. Nuts look like 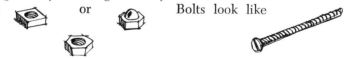 or   Bolts look like

But the real facts are, you will hardly ever need nuts or bolts to build something, just to fix it. Usually it's the nut that somehow has disappeared. It mostly gets lost from places like tubular-metal chairs, bar stools, cribs, TV and kitchen carts.

Picture Hangers. I've never thought much of the glue-on fabric hangers, although they are easy to use. One section pastes on the wall, the other to the picture back. Then all you do is hook the two together. They're OK for real lightweight hangings, or worth the try if you have a wall-obsessed landlord. Better, and not all that crater-making in the wall, are the standard metal hangers   . These come in graduated sizes, the small holding up to 10 lbs. and going all the way up to real heavyweights (100 lbs.). Of this type, the ones I dearly love cost more, but the rewards of no-bending nails, unobtrusive hanger parts and a sunnier disposition for the installer make them worthwhile. The nail part has a sapphire head with a needle-sharp steel shaft. The hanger part looks like   or   (for heavier pictures).

Sandpaper. Think of your finger-nail emery board and you've got the picture. The coarser side grinds off while the fine side smooths. Sand-paper, of course, isn't made with sand any more. It just feels like it. The degree of coarseness is graded by number—the higher the num-ber, the finer the sanding texture—except for emery (for sanding metal), whose numbering system mysteriously goes the other way. Mercifully, most of the kinds you'll be using will also be labeled fine, medium and coarse. Honestly, though, if you just go by feel you'll probably do fine. Err on the side of too fine and go coarser if you need to, rather than gouge tracks in spackling repairs or softer woods like pine. Sand *with* the wood grain, not across.

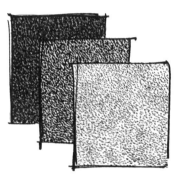

Screws, Wood. Let's clear up one thing fast. The adjective here does not describe the screw itself but what you use it in, with the exception of lead and plastic fasteners (page 16). All screws are metal of some sort: aluminum, brass or steel mostly, and are categorized by length and diameter. They are flat-headed 🔩 , roundheaded 🔩 , and slightly round-headed 🔩 , either with a single slot as shown or a star-shaped one ⊕🔩 that takes the Phillips screwdriver (page 12). This last type is easiest for us girls. The screwdriver tends to lock into place and doesn't slip off as you turn it. There are other nuances to screws, such as the shape of the backside of the head. For instance, the flat backside will screw flush to the surface but the head will show. The tapered backside is designed so that the head ends up flush with the surface. Since your choice depends on the individual use, we'll pick that up as we go along.

Silicone Coaters are new-fangled lubricants, either in tube or spray can, which make doors, drawers and almost anything that's supposed to slide, slide. They are available in many brand names— all of them good. One word of caution: If you're using the spray in a downward direction, spread a newspaper on the area below. The "drift" of the spray will make the floors slidy, too.

Sneakers. These are an absolute must for projects, unless you have prehensile toes. Even then a prehensile, barefoot-prone friend of mine got blown clean off an aluminum stepstool while simply wiping (with a damp cloth) the top of her air conditioner. This goes for TV sets, too. Besides insulating

you, sneakers give you mountain-goat-footedness for some of the balancing acts you may attempt on bathtub edges or other spots where you *shouldn't* try but will. Another word of caution: Sneakers can be sneaky. The soles smooth out long before the canvas top goes. They're cheap insurance. Buy a new pair for projects and wear the beat-up beauties elsewhere.

Steel Wool. This comes in three grades: fine, medium and coarse. As creepy as it feels, steel wool is indispensable as a shiner-up and taker-off. Almost always, "fine" is the grade for you.

Stepladder. Get one! It makes projects easier and is much safer than tempting alternates like chairs and hassocks and the bathroom tub—even with sneakers. You don't have to go whole hog and get a for-real one unless you have high ceilings, big paint jobs (see page 136) and nobody to borrow from. Storage is quite a problem for these bigger ladders. A good versatile type I've found, about 40″ high, looks like the one shown. Two points to recommend it are the wide steps, which help your balance, and the curved support bar, which gives your legs some-

thing to lean against when you're on the top step and reaching.

Tape, Electrical. A must to keep short circuits out of the electrical side of your life. It's actually an insulating tape to wrap around the exposed portions of metal wiring. For the how and where it's used, see Electricity (page 65).

Tape, Masking. The double-faced kind is great for attaching light-weight objects on verticals, and heavier things on the horizontal. One, for instance, is Carpet Squares (page 103). You simply stick on a piece of the tape on either the object or the surface. Then peel off the top paper layer, which exposes a nice sticky strip.

Toolbox. My first came as a birthday present along with a black lace slip. A toolbox is a neat, noisy organizer for keeping and carrying your tools. Until you have a collection, an airline flight bag is a sturdy substitute. Matter of fact, I still use an El Al pouch for my electric drill.

Walls, Types of. This may sound dull, but it can make "going to the wall" a much simpler, less frustrating experience if you know what you are facing. In some cases, knowing what you're up against may keep you from getting into the experience in the first place. There can be awful problems!

HOLLOW construction is usually found in inside walls and once in a while in outside walls of newer buildings. In older buildings, chances are that all walls will be hollow. As ominous as this may sound, all it means is that there is space behind the wall surface you see. The wall may be made of layers of finish plaster, rough plaster and a lath of wood or metal wire. The lath (a supporting base for plaster) is attached to the studs which are the basic vertical supports of the wall. In good construction the studs are spaced about 16″ or so apart, but these days, don't count on it.

Another hollow-wall construction is called drywall, which is either plasterboard or gypsum or Sheetrock. To me, and for our purposes, they are all one and the same. To the experts I'm sure there is a difference. Drywall comes in sheets, panels or boards—again take your choice of terms—and is nailed directly to the studs. With the demise of plastering as an art, this form of construction is being increasingly used because it's fast, economical,

straight and smooth. Unfortunately, it's about as soundproof as a tuning fork.

SOLID walls are the words which pretty much tell the story. Usually this refers to a wall built of cinder block, brick, concrete or stone. It can be covered with plaster to give a smooth-wall appearance. You're liable to run into this on outside walls and in between apartment walls.

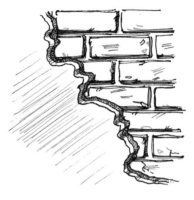

Count your many blessings if the hollow wall is your lot. Even cinder block is worth a small cheer. The trick with brick is to drill into and insert the fastener in the mortar in between the brick. It's stronger than the brick, anyway. Concrete and stone—sob! sob!—almost always require professional help (see page 52).

Wood.

LUMBER is wood cut to various lengths, widths and thicknesses graded by quality. For most of your projects, you'll probably be dealing with pine. It's inexpensive, easy to work with, and takes stain or paint very well. However, buy a good grade of pine to avoid big, gummy knots, flaws and excessive warping. We'll worry about the other woods as they come up in special projects, like finishing unfinished furniture (see page 118). The really goofy thing about lumber is the so-called size of it. A 2″ x 4″ (that's depth and width, not length) is no more a 2″ x 4″ than I'm a ten-foot pine tree. It's been 1 ⅝″ x 3 ⅝″ for some time. The official explanation for this discrepancy is shrinkage or "aging." The last I heard, our friendly lumber companies were trying to reduce the size, not the price, still further, to 1 ½" x 3 ½". The same discrepant sizes apply to other dimensions too. For instance, a 10" board is 9 ⅝", 8" is 7 ⅝", and so on. Unless you're building or putting in some masterpiece that has to fit exactly, it's not a problem. Otherwise, beware and compensate accordingly.

PLYWOOD is wood processed in thin layers placed at right angle by grain to create a strong, warp-resistant material. Again 1" thick isn't 1" here either—it's ⅞". Plywood comes in panels so that you can get an "unbroken" surface much wider than that possible with regular lumber. Most lumber yards will cut plywood to the size you want. The grain and raw edges of plywood always put me off. Freud would say I'm reminded of the day before tourist cabins became motels. However, modern-day veneers, stripping and coverings do well in changing that image. In fact, they have changed so much that in some cases you have to keep a sharp eye out to be sure the solid walnut whosis you're paying for is really solid walnut.

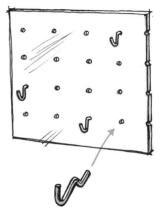

HARDBOARD is finely ground wood fibers mightily compressed under heat. To make it easy for you to spot, it's smooth (sometimes on one side only) and hard, and what pegboard is made from. Its uniformly-spaced holes and special hooks allow you to hang anything that will hang, like pots, pans, utensils, shelves, tools, memos, pictures and what-not. Pegboard is invaluable for wall storage in champed quarters with little cupboard and drawer space around. Regular holeless hardboard sawed to size makes good cabinet dividers for records, mounts for photos, prints or posters. All types come in big sheets which you can have cut to size, or you can usually find close-to-size scraps at your lumberyard.

MOLDING and STRIPS can be found in multitudinous shapes and sizes. The more common ones are:

They work wonders as cheap picture frames, shelf and table edges, or joint and seam coverers. (More about this later.)

How to Follow Directions (except some)

Most directions seem to have been printed by manufacturers who must have a profitable sideline inscribing the Lord's Prayer on the head of a pin. This same small type is usually used on the small size container that's most economical and practical for you. It's also the type that's almost always the most important to read. So get your glasses and/or a bright light—and read.

Never, never ignore the warnings! Manufacturers are loath to put them on the item in the first place. If they're there, you can be sure the warnings are as important as they sound. Probably more so. Some of the ones to watch out for are:

FLAMMABLE AND INFLAMMABLE!

For some peculiar nonreason these contradictory words mean exactly the same thing—fire making! Generally, you'll find this warning on wax, varnish, lacquer, shellac, alcohol, turpentine, paint thinner, paint remover, kerosene, rubber cement, glue, and the like. The invisible fumes are what catch fire more than the actual stuff (that's what VOLATILE means—and keep an eye out for that word, too), so if you're a smoker, be extra careful. A side effect can be "headiness" if you inhale the fumes over a prolonged period—even in an unstuffy room.

USE IN WELL VENTILATED ROOM!

This warning almost always accompanies the previous one on labels. However, the exception is carbon tetrachloride, nicknamed carbon tet. Widely hailed as a nonflammable, efficient, inexpensive "dry" cleaner, carbon tet can be downright lethal. I know of one woman who cleaned her living-room carpet without opening the windows. Even though this was in a house where the air could circulate, she *died* about two hours later. Only recently has the government moved to make the sale of carbon tet illegal. If you have any hanging around the house, do yourself a favor and get rid of it. Replace it with one of the new products similar to those used by commercial cleaners. Ask your druggist or hardware-store man to recommend one. Whatever product you're using, carbon tet or not, and whether you have a window to open or not—if your project goes on, get out of the room every once in a while to clear your head.

CAUSTIC!

This means the product can severely burn, eat, even destroy tissue. Sweetie, that's skin, eyes and all that belongs to you. Paint removers and many oven and drain cleaners are the best-known of the caustic breed. (In fact, if they're too "safe," they usually don't work all that effectively. Fortunately, there's no mistaking when some spills on you; you know it. Immediately wash off the burning spot with plenty of cold or lukewarm water and no damage will be done. If your eye's involved, don't go searching for an eye cup and 5% boric acid water. Either get your head directly under the kitchen faucet or make your own eye cup out of your palm to hold the running water, and force the water up against the eyeball. Overdo it with the water. To be on the safe side, check with your doctor as soon as you can. But better yet, avoid the possibility by being smart in the first place and wear glasses (see page 19), even sun glasses if that's all you have.

POISON!

Often this word accompanies other warnings which sometimes point up the dangers of inhaling or swallowing the product. Since I've discussed inhaling (i.e., carbon tet), the following is about swallowing. If someone accidentally swallows a poisonous liquid you'll probably panic—I would, so I won't say "Don't!" Try to calm down enough to do two things.

First, with package in hand, call for help. Naturally, if you've swallowed the poison and others are with you, have them do the calling. Call your doctor, police emergency number or better yet, if you have one, a poison information center. These centers are trained to deal with the wide variety of poisons in their numerous forms. They can give you the best, immediate advice.

Second, no matter whom you call, while you're waiting for the phone to be answered, start to read the specific antidote on the label. Then, if for some reason you get no answer or help will be some time in coming, you can begin remedial action.

One very important reason for reading the antidote on the label is that by training and nature, the first thing most humans think of is vomiting to get rid of any distressing substance. With many, many poisons this is the worst thing you can do. For instance, caustics can burn away tissue as much coming up as they do going down. Another poison is a product like lighter fluid, which contains a petroleum distillate. If you vomit, its volatile characteristics could cause respiratory problems, possibly pneumonia. Insecticides can fall into the latter group, or in what most of us think of as "true" poison like arsenic. In these cases, vomiting is likely to be recommended, but the label should tell you what's "safe" to do and how to do it. None of this sounds nice but it is necessary. Knowing what to do could save you from serious injury, even death. Hopefully, you will get professional help from the start or at some point along the way, either by phone or in person. Treat the immediate poison problem by following the instructions on the label, and then follow up with either a call or a visit to a doctor.

TOXIC!

Actually this is an adjective meaning poisonous, but it's sometimes printed in big letters all by itself. Although "toxic" sounds like a step-down in lethalness, it is just as potent, so watch out for it. If affected either internally or externally, follow the appropriate directions discussed.

Now to following the *directions* themselves. They may be gobbledygook, misleading, confusing, overpromising, boring, but you will get some facts and functions straight from them. As your confidence and expertise build, you'll know what and when to disregard. As you wend your way through this book, you'll find it loaded with ifs, buts, sometimeses, maybes, most-of-the-timeses, usuallys, especiallys, particularlys, then agains, probablys and possiblys. But that's the way of the fixit world. Almost nothing (right off I can't think of one thing) ever goes as marvelously well as the directions direct. Just like cooking frozen vegetables or stirring up a cake mix, the project at hand always takes a little longer, is a touch harder and the results not quite as spectacular as promised. So be it, that's a good deal of what this book's for—how to take up the gap between theory and reality. Most important—use the directions to figure out what you're trying to do, so when something goofs or you do, with the help of the following hard-won advice you can work it out.

Figuring & Fixing

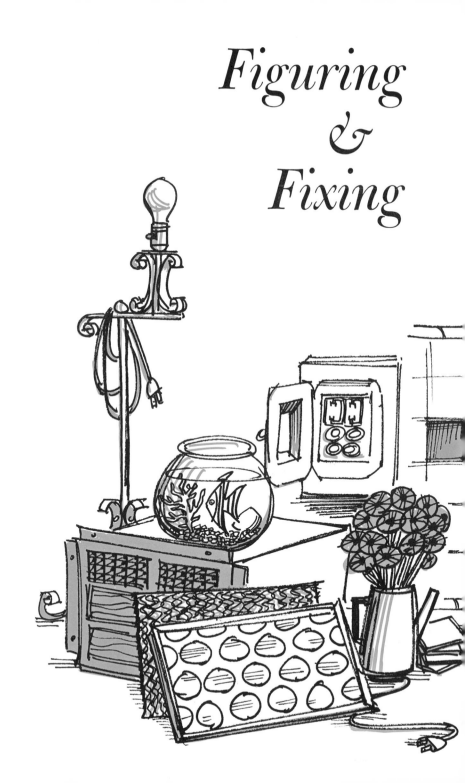

or How to

Make the Place

Livable

Projects covered here are probably more pedestrian than provocative. Although I must say I've gotten rather provoked doing some of these jobs, they're the kind you know are lurking there, always waiting for *somebody* to do *something*. Face up to it—you win (or lose), as the case might be. The big hurdle for most of us, after inertia is overcome, is finding the nerve to actually start something we've never done before. Be heartened! Women's mechanical dexterity was proved statistically way back in World War II. They outshone the boys in manufacturing and assembling all sorts of complicated whatsits. So much for the mystique of the handy man. If you can read a recipe, and many of them are more involved than what we're dealing with here, you can wire a lamp, change a washer and turn a hand at all sorts of things when you put your mind to it. Put on the old track shoes (sneakers in this case) and away we go!

Air-Conditioner Filters. About the clearest directions in most air-conditioner manuals are how to get at the filters. With some units you need an engineering degree to learn how to turn them on. But, air pollution being what it is, for your unit to work well and in some cases to prevent it from "icing up" (similar to your freezer), filters should be checked, cleaned or replaced fairly often. Following the directions,

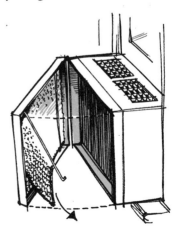

peer at the filter. If it looks rather
dirty and hairy, proceed to remove
it from the unit. I've dealt with
several different kinds of air conditioners, and it seems to me that the
filters fall into two groups. There's
the flexible-sheet form either of thin
foamy or fibrous material or something that looks like mail (that's the
metallic tunic that made knights'
chests chestier). This type of filter is
either held in place by spring wires
or is hung from hooks. The second
kind of filter can be of the above
materials or spun-glass fibers, but
it's contained in a rigid frame and
looks much like a window venti-
lator. This filter usually slides in and
out of slots.

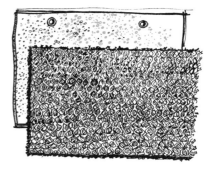

All of these can be removed,
vacuumed and/or washed. However, if the filter is looking be-
draggled or doesn't seem to clean
well, take it in hand (it's not heavy)
and buy a new one exactly like it.
Check out "Filters, Air Condition-
ing" in the Yellow Pages or try the
hardware store or the equivalent
section at larger department stores.
Believe me, taking the filter along
can save light-years of time and
explanations.

Antenna, TV—Hook Up. Since almost all sets except the big
consoles now come with built-in antenna, the rabbit ears of
yesteryear are not multiplying. Most of the time these built-ins

do as well as or better than the master antenna that many apartment houses feature. One reason for this is that a master antenna, if it's worth anything in the first place, has to be maintained. It's not a simple little metal thing waving bravely in the wind. It has components that need periodic checkups and service. I found out this truth in one building where my TV picture rolled wildly (on certain channels) unless I disconnected my set from the master antenna, raised the Venetian blind and sat in a direct line with the Empire State Building. This was a bit of a bore and hard on the eyes, since it meant sitting on the edge of the bed in an alcove some twenty-two feet away. Believing it had to be a problem with the set, I finally called a TV serviceman. I explained to him how I had managed to stop the rolling. Then he explained (nervously, as if I were some kind of a nut) about the master antenna. A year or so later, with a different set and a different apartment, I called the same serviceman to solve a different problem. He kept looking over his shoulder and muttering, "Haven't I met you some place before?" Who, me?

If you want to try to hook into the master antenna, first pull the plug of the set. Look on the back of the set for a small fiberboard panel with screws and wires hooked to them. You may find more than one set of screws and wires. Disconnect the wires from the screws marked VHF. Push these wires out of the way, keeping them separated. Connect an appropriate length of TV cable bought at the TV store to these screws, and the other end to the wall master-antenna outlet.

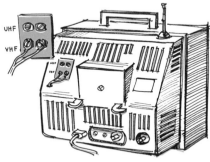

The catch or catches are as follows: Not all sets label VHF and UHF; not all sets put the fiberboard panel on the back; some outlets take a single plug instead of two wires.

The installation can be a breeze or a shambles. If you have any questions, ask your TV or electronics store before you invest.

Bathroom Fixtures

SHOWER HEAD. By taking it with me, I've had a good shower head in the last three places I've lived. Some landlords with Scrooge-like personalities supply the tinniest heads around. To change your shower head for another, remove the one you have. Look for a hexagonal collar nut, which is either on the back of the shower head or somewhere on the pipe that comes out of the wall. Put tape on the nut and use a wrench (see page 14) to loosen it. If it's frozen (that's pro talk for "won't budge"), don't wrench with too much vim or you may break something. Put a few drops of oil or rust dissolver on it and wait about an hour or so, then try again.

When you get it off, take it with you to the hardware or plumbing store. This ensures getting the right fit on the pipe, or an adapter to make it so. Buy the head that matches your psyche, put it on and tuck the other away till moving day, then replace.

SOAP DISHES, PAPER HOLDERS, ETC., *see* TOWEL RACKS

TOILET SEATS. Way back when—when I first outlined this book I obviously was going to tell you something deathless about toilet seats. For the life of me, I can't think what it was or even why. I suspect the thought was that if you were saddled with a cheap plastic seat and you wanted a gay, bright place to park, you can manage it much like the shower-head routine—or buy your own and store the landlord's. The only figuring you have to do is the shape of the seat in relation to the bowl. For instance, if you have the standard oval bowl, the wide elongated seat won't fit. With this in mind, buy a new seat, store the other (under the bed is interesting) and when you move replace it and take the pretty one with you.

Installation of the new seat is a snap. The nuts and bolts (plastic these days), or big neoprene expansion bolts come right with the seat and line up with the holes in the bowl. Rust may make getting the old nuts and bolts off difficult. Maybe that's the reason for this section!

One funny, awful story of a guy who was trying to replace his toilet seat. The nuts had rusted on the bolts. Instead of using a hacksaw to saw through the bolts above the nuts (some you can't, because of indentations in the bowl), or a rust dissolver, he opted for a hammer and a screwdriver. Disaster struck when he struck the screwdriver. It slipped and he hit the tank with the hammer. Big hole! Big waterfall! And guess what?—no cut-off valve and no sense to hold up the tank float! (See page 88.)

Bathroom Tiles

CLEANING. If you just didn't take baths and showers, tiles would be no problem. Certainly all of them have to be washed down occasionally, but that's a snap compared to the tub and shower section. Of course, if you "clean" the tile every day as recommended by the manufacturers, this section need not concern you. But us normal types only realize how dirty the tile is just before company comes. Despite the glowing promises of "Now, New, At Last," I've yet to find a tile cleaner that performs as grandly as advertised. Until I do, it's good old-fashioned kerosene for me. A moon-lighting fireman tipped me off on this fast, easy solution. It's flammable (or in-), so don't smoke, open a window if you can and be prepared to remove the slight film it leaves on the tile with detergent and water. Kerosene is also cheap. In cities you can usually get it at hardware stores; in the hinterlands, a gas station is your best bet. If the seams around the tile are really urky, take an old toothbrush and some scouring powder to them. Alas! it's the only good way.

REPLACING. If a wall tile loosens or falls out—unfortunately some tile setters have slipshod ways—you can buy suitable adhesive to stick it back on at most paint or hardware stores. Scrape or chip as much of the old adhesive off the back of the tile as you can. A relatively even surface is what you're after.

Spread a thin coat of the new adhesive on the back of the tile and press it back in place. If more than one tile has fallen out, try to space them so that they line up with others. The adhesive will usually set tight in about twelve hours, more or less if the directions say so. Check the directions, particularly if you're working in wet or about-to-be-wet areas. Next is grout time. Grout is

the white filler around tile. You can buy grout at the same time as the adhesive, unless you like exercise or the man behind the counter. Mix the grout per instructions on the container to about the consistency of thick mayonnaise. Force the mixture into the seams either with your finger or a putty knife. For big areas, I use my window-washer squeegee (it was never that great for windows—now it's worse), dragging it crisscross over the surface. Check for "skips," little areas where the grout doesn't fill in. Then use a Turkish towel or washcloth and wipe off the grout on the surface of the tile with a fairly heavy hand. This forces the grout into the seams and gets rid of the excess as well. Wait for about fifteen minutes and wipe the tile clean with a damp sponge. In about five minutes, if a white haze has re-formed on the tile, mop again. If the haze really sets before you get at it, it's razor-blade scraping time—so keep an eye on it and save yourself some work.

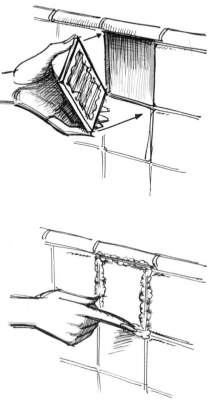

SEALING, OR CAULKING. This is the same breed of cats as grouting, only here you are working to seal where the wall tile meets the tub, and/or shower. There are special waterproof compounds packaged in tubes for easy application. I guess it's easy. Maybe it's me, but my results never look quite as shipshape as those pictured in the directions. You're supposed to squeeze the tube continuously with the same force and move it along the area at the same pace—straight, too! If you falter, and I do when my hand gets tired, the results are uneven. When you go back to fix up an uneven spot, it gets messy. However, persevere because water seepage can cause all sorts of complications—mildew, germs, bugs, wet plaster, rotting wood.

There is also vinyl tape that is "easily" installed around the fixture edges. In theory, this should be the ideal sealing solution. However, until the manufacturer gets some of the "bugs" out of the product, I wouldn't recommend what it does for your disposition or the problem. The mop-like applicator for putting on the adhesive is cheap, badly designed and too big to go in and out of the bottle easily. The tape itself twists and curls. To me, even with two working, it was like trying to put nail polish on a snake. The twisting tape makes it impossible to get a complete and even seal all the way around. I've seen four finished jobs in the last year, and in every instance there are loose spots where the water can seep through.

A more permanent solution and, I think, a better one is a tile kit with enough quarter round tiles to seal around the average tub. They come in black, white and standard tile colors. The directions for installation are clear and easy to follow. These kits are available from mail-order houses and some hardware stores.

Blinds, Venetian. If you're mad for Chinese ring puzzles, I leave the dismantling, retaping and restringing to you. Ah so! Marco Polo *did* find them first in China, didn't he? So be it. Most of us are saddled with them, and at least in city apartments they get filthy fast. The drawbacks of sending them out for cleaning are cost (the landlord's supposed to do this at lease time but in between times you're stuck) and time. Ten days to two weeks is a long while to sleep in public and hide in closets. My solution, horrible as it is, is the bathtub shower! Buy a heavy-duty cleaner, not so heavy (or dilute more) if your blinds are wood, because some of these cleaners will take the hide off the proverbial elephant.

To remove the blinds from the windows, pull the blind up tight to the top and disengage the metal bands on each end from the little metal points that hold them, and flip up. "Flip up" is probably far too simple a direction. In rentals, most of these metal ends have been mangled or endlessly painted over. These handicaps make for a real finger-nail-breaking or finger-cutting exercise. The best answer is to use a small screwdriver and gently try to pry the band loose and up. Often this loosening is a pulling action and there's not much of an edge on the metal ends to pull against. Be careful. Too hearty an effort may send you over backward off the ladder. Slide the blind out toward you and head for the bathtub.

For the blinds that will fit lengthwise in the tub or even on an angle close to the top, draw enough hot water to cover and add cleaner. The more water, the more cleaner. You want a strong mix. Hold the blind up and release the cord so that the blind comes down as much as possible. Lower it into the filled tub. Leave it to soak for about a half-hour. Since the slats love to stick together, stir once in a while if you can. Then take a soft brush, old washcloth or paper-type kitchen cloth and work your way through, slat by slat. It's not hard, just messy, tedious—and watch the edges. They can be cutting. After you finish, empty the tub and turn on the shower. (You'll need to, anyway, to get rid of the silt—that says something about my housekeeping!) Pull the blind up through the spray, then loosely roll it up and lean it against the end for draining.

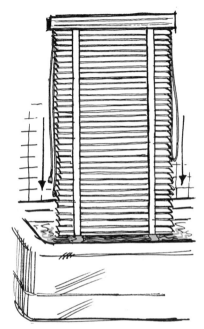

For larger-sized blinds, too big to fit lengthwise in the tub, take them down the same way, but first mix a bucketful of a really strong concentration of cleaner and put it with brush or cloth in the tub or as close as possible to it. With the blind, make one stop on your way to the tub. Take off your clothes—this is a shower skirmish. Get yourself and the blind into the tub. Open the blind just enough to be able to free the slats, then turn on the shower. Start scrubbing; again watch the cutting edges. This is somewhat akin to wrestling a metal alligator or "Nude Descending a Staircase," but at least you wash and rinse at the same time. I recommend you do this before your visit to the hairdresser. Drain as above. A fifteen-minute draining is usually sufficient to get most of the water out of the way. Put the blinds back up. If you want to protect your window sills and can't remove the ends of the bottom hollow bar where extra water collects, cover the sills with paper or Turkish towels to catch the leftover drips.

A slower but more dependable and less athletic way to clean the larger blinds is to use a plastic paint-drop cloth. Remove the blind as before, only don't pull it up to the top. Leave it extended and lay the blind on the floor on top of the waterproof paint-drop cloth. Take a bucket of cleaning solution and a soft cloth and wash the blind, slat by slat. Keep the action on the dry side or you'll have a problem keeping the water on the cloth.

Carpet Cleaning. The professional take-it-up-and-out cleaners do a better job than you can do. But here again, the time, cost and inconvenience are big factors. And, of course, there's always the wall-to-wall problem, too. The "dry" cleaners or foam sprays are adequate and better than putting off any cleaning for the above reasons.

Far better and surprisingly easy is the electrical shampooer (you can buy or rent one). In fact, I think you can do as good a job or better than the services that come in, and much less expensively. You care more and can do the square footage you want to do when you want to do it.

Rejoice! The instruction books I've seen with these machines are good and easy to follow. Since each shampooer has its own little quirks, the specific booklet that comes with it is better than any general directions I could give. Basically, though, the idea is not to stay too long in one spot. Keep moving. Let the suds do the work, and the less wet the rug becomes, the better. If furniture has to be moved back while the carpet is still damp (do you know anyone who has so much space that she doesn't have to do this?), cut squares of leftover rug pad or even rug, something heavy and springy. Then wrap the pieces in aluminum foil. The heavy material cushions the load, and the foil prevents rusting from the slides on the bottom of the furniture.

Curtain/Drapery Rods, Traverse or Otherwise. Urk! Blah! Yuk! The job nominated to hate most. Here's one that if you can con anybody, even George himself—con. But alas! Almost anyone who's ever been through putting up rods will experience catatonic symptoms and withdraw. If you're renting and the rods are UP and even close to the height and length you want, be firm about them staying put when you move in. Under most leases, rods fall into the category of "permanently attached." Barring that luck, my best advice is to go ahead and be willing to cheat, swear, cry and settle for almost anything as long as you get the rods to stay up. To keep this chore from being even more cumbersome, I'll use draperies to stand for curtains, too.

The problems are legion. First, the fixtures themselves must have been designed, and never improved, in the year '01 when windows had wide wood frames and nobody ever dreamed of going beyond them. The screws supplied with the rods are P-pitiful, barely adequate for

wood and never wide or strong
enough to expand the anchors and
shields needed in most apartment
wall installations. The "holes" in the
wall brackets for the screws are
somewhat less accessible than the
entry to King Tut's tomb. The holes
on the back of the bracket are bad
enough but at least you can see
them. The side holes described
blithely as "you can also use this
bracket on the side walls for wall-
to-wall installation" are nigh on to
impossible.

Before you buy rods, figure out
the width and length of the draperies you want. You'll probably
have to order them. Rare is the day
you can walk into a store and find
them to your specifications. Don't
necessarily limit yourself to the window measurements. With a little
pre-thought and imagination you
can go up, down and sideways.
For ready-made draperies, you
work with lengths of 54", 63",
72", 96" and 108" and usually 1, 2 or
3 widths.

If you're going all-out for custom-made draperies, the store will
adjust to your wishes. However, take your window measurements,
as well as your proposed drapery measurements, with you. You
may find that by altering your measurements by a couple inches
one way or another, you can save a lot of money by not having to
buy extra lengths of material.

Before I forget and you do, too—make sure you allow enough
material to cover the end or sides of the bracket. Counting both

ends usually adds about 6″ to your drapery width. This is not necessary when you want your draperies to go from wall to wall.

Buy rods so that the drapery measurements are well within the maximum length described on the label of the rod. For example, don't use a 48″ to 84″ rod for 84″-width draperies; use a 66″ to 120″ rod. Stretching the rods too close to the maximum width of your draperies will only lead to sagging. Besides, for this struggle you need all the maneuvering room you can manage.

To put up back wall brackets, measure equal distances from each side of the window opening in a line with the top of the window. If you want the rod above the window line, then measure the appropriate distance up on each side. If the rods are long, measure for a center brace, or if the rod is extra long and/or the draperies are heavy, two equally spaced braces. These brackets should be at right angles to the wall.

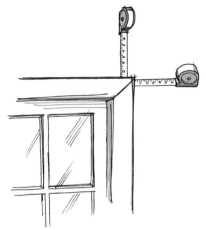

For side wall-to-wall installation, prepare for the worst. If your side walls are by some miracle at honest right angles to the end wall, then you only have to fight the bad design of the fixture. This isn't so bad; the fixture can be subdued. However, most walls being what they are will go off at a slight angle. Again, the brackets and the rod must be at right angles. Even a couple of degrees off on the side wall will tend to make the screws pull out. To correct this, you need a shim. Technically, this is a wedge, usually of wood. If you can't find any wood shaped to the angle needed to put things right, or aren't much of a whittler, I've found matchbooks work just fine.

Hold the bracket against the wall and ring the holes with a pencil. Don't forget—since you want the drapery heading to cover the rod—that the placement of the rod determines where the bottom of the drapery will hang. Position the bracket so that when the rod is installed, it (or the plastic hangers on the rod) will line up with the spots where you want the hooks on the heading of the draperies. Drill holes in the wall using a masonry bit (see page 13) of the necessary diameter. Although there are usually five holes in the back of the brackets, I've found after various disasters that two or three (as numbered in the illustration) almost always will hold. Start there. In their infinite wisdom the designers have made the holes very close together. Often when you drill, the side-by-side holes run together and you have one big hole (see Disasters—How to Recoup and Overcome, page 53). Easy does it.

From here on, although we've been talking curtain-rod installation, the same techniques, materials and frustrations will apply to most other wall installations of everything from can openers to bookshelves. Where there are exceptions or better ways, they'll be noted under the specific project.

If the masonry bit, after you've been grinding away, suddenly "goes through," *voilà!* You're dealing with hollow wall construction and can use Mollys or plastic anchors that will blossom behind the wall for solid footing.

If you plan to do this project when the stores are closed, buy fasteners of various sizes. You can always return them, but I've found that a stock of fasteners quickly dispatches many a spur-of-the-moment inspiration. To determine the length of fastener you need, check the bit. Plaster tends to stick in the grooves of the bit, so where the plaster line stops is where you broke through and Q.E.D. the depth of the hole. You simply measure from the end of the bit to the plaster line to get the right size of fastener.

If the bit just keeps grinding away but still makes progress, you're dealing with a solid wall. This calls for plugs or shields (see page 16). Make the hole deeper than the fasteners. These plugs and shields expand against the side of the hole, so should fit snugly when tapped in with a hammer. If you're using lead shields, don't whack them. They're soft and will bend or flatten. They often do this anyway just to be difficult, so always buy extras.

If the bit has been drilling with results and suddenly hits something solid (you'll know), you've got problems. Chances are you've met up with steel or poured concrete. Despair, despair—unless the hole is at least ½" deep, then you can cheat (see page 55).

If the hole is shallower, there are some solutions that have worked for me. You may be too close to the window edge and have run into the steel frame that's buried in the wall. If you're working near or on the ceiling it could be a steel beam. Move somewhat away from the area and see what happens. This is most likely to happen in newer buildings. Don't assume that because you run into a problem in one place, it will hold true elsewhere, even on the same line. Once I put up a traverse rod with Mollys on the left end, a wood plug (see page 55) in the center and lead shields on the right. It's crazy—so keep exploring and experimenting. There's always spackling to hide the unsuccessful holes.

Before you start, it's a good idea to ask the previous tenant, neighbor or super what problems they had or what kind of construction the building has. Poured concrete is impossible to penetrate with a hand drill; the same is true of an electric drill (you'll burn out the motor) unless you have a gadget (expensive) that slows the electric drill's speed. It takes a slow, steady, strong force to eventually cut through. Unless you're noted for your biceps, I wouldn't recommend trying. If you know you're going to face trouble, buy the curtain rod in a store that will send a muscle man to install it. Of course, there are apartments—I know of two in New York City—where the handyman actually will do it.

DISASTERS—HOW TO RECOUP AND OVERCOME

Hole is too big. Start over in a different spot, but still in line with measurements, and spackle in the bad one later. If the hole isn't too huge or irregular, you may be able to use a larger size of fastener than planned for and get it to catch. Barring that, here are some things to try:

Fill in the hole with a Spackle- or putty-type filler and insert the fastener while the filler is wet. Don't even attempt to screw into it for a few days or it will pull out or turn right along with the screw. If the other screws are holding securely and company's beating a path to your door, go ahead and install the fixture, then finish the one that didn't work later on. In the meantime, treat the fixture gingerly.

Place the fastener in the hole and then force small pieces of wood in around it. Push them in the depth of the hole and then snap off the heads even with the wall surface. Wooden kitchen matches are great. If you're using "strike anywhere" matches, strike them elsewhere first. What you're really looking for is anything that will give the fasteners something to hang on to and, in turn, will grip the sides of the hole despite weight and pull. A little Spackle or water putty mixed in with the wood pieces never hurts. Another solution may be wood plugs (see page 55).

With hollow walls, the too-big hole is sometimes not as difficult to fix as in solid walls. The mushrooming action of the Molly will solve the rear problem. Unless you have a crater, it will expand bigger than the hole. What you need is a firm wall surface for the front end of the Molly to "seat" itself against. You can fill in the hole with a Spackle-type compound and wait for it to harden. With a razor-blade knife or saw, you can cut a small square of thin wood slightly larger than the hole. Drill a hole in the wood to match the diameter of the sleeve of the Molly. Place it over the disaster area, slip the Molly through and proceed. Rubber or soft plastic washers, depending on the size of the hole, can work instead.

Shield turns with screw. If the screw and shield turn around and around together and you don't hear a slight grating sound of metal against masonry, this means the fastener is too small for the hole. Use the next larger size.

If you continue to hear a grating sound, stop right there. You're probably reaming out the hole, and the shield isn't catching. Chances are that the screw is too big for the hole in the shield. You're expecting it to cut through too much lead as it threads its way. Select a screw smaller in diameter. If you haven't stopped soon enough, you may have made the hole too big for your fastener. Either get a larger size shield or do the match-stick bit around the sides (page 53).

Another possibility is that the insides of the wall (under the finish plaster) are just plain bad. Shoddy construction is usually the villain in newer buildings, while too many years may be the cause in older buildings. I had never hit this problem until I moved into a building put up around 1930. To my dismay, the seemingly marvelous, uncracked, real plaster walls had feet of sand. Charlie, the best super in the memory of living woman, clued me in. His advice to me, and mine to you, is to forget the anchors, etc., and use a wood plug.

Find a stick-type piece of wood at the lumberyard or ask your liquor dealer for a wine crate. Whittle a piece of wood to approximately hole size. Drill the hole in the wall as deep as you can. If possible, keep going until you hit solid backing underneath, like brick or cinder block. Force the wood into the hole until it stops. Pound it in to be sure. Then take a hacksaw blade, without the benefit of the frame, and saw off the wood sticking out to make it even with the wall. Simply attach the fixture with wood screws.

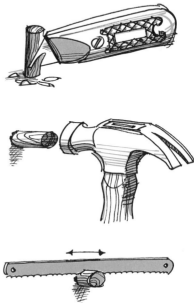

Anchor or shield works out of the hole. Pure and simple, the screw's too long for the fastener and the hole you've drilled. The screw has gone through the back of the fastener and hit something solid—too solid. What's happening is that the fastener is working its way back up the screw threading, literally being pushed out of the hole. Start over with a shorter screw.

Hole is too shallow. Here's the cheat I referred to earlier (see page 52). Use wire clippers to cut off part of the back of a lead shield. Since this will squash the fastener somewhat, use the pliers to get it back to near roundness. Put the shield in the hole and smack it with a hammer. Smacking tends to flatten the shield inside and out. This flattening, combined with a very short screw, usually works and will hold up lighter objects, such as toothbrush holders and the center brace of a curtain rod where little strain occurs. I don't recommend it for places where it has to carry a heavier load.

If any of the fixtures pull down after they seem to be up solidly, chances are that one of the remedial actions suggested will correct the problem. Ingenuity and pure bullheadedness is the name of the game. Remember, you're looking for something that these fasteners can sink their teeth into. Look around and think—your own version of first aid may be staring right at you. One friend of mine has found that steel wool stuffed in the hole or around the screw takes a good bite and holds well.

❊   ❊   ❊

Doors. If doors don't stay shut, if they sag, stick a little or squeak a lot, you can usually alleviate the problem without resorting to extreme measures, like calling for outside help.

The squeak is the easiest to correct. It's metal rubbing on metal 99 percent of the time. In other words, the hinges need oil, or more contemporarily, a silicone coater. If the hinge is so encrusted with paint as to make the squeak inaccessible, take the measures suggested on page 107.

When the door sticks or doesn't stay shut, too much paint is almost always the reason. Paint over the latch and catch (these should never be painted but almost always are) means the lock can't work freely, if at all. An accumulation on the edges of the door and frame means too tight a fit. In either case, get rid of the excess paint. The really thick coats can be chipped or scraped off or decimated with paint remover (see page 114). Lesser layers can be done away with by placing and holding a piece of rough sandpaper on the area and closing and opening the door several times. If you have a solid-wood door, a plane can be used. Top and side, only, unless you take the door completely off.

Occasionally sticking is caused when there is not enough paint to seal the wood against moisture. The wood swells and causes sticking. The sandpaper or plane treatment works here. Then seal with a light coat of paint.

Severe sagging happens most often when everything is out of

line, thanks to termites, bad construction, settling or plain old age. Sounds almost human doesn't it?

It can also be the result of loose screws in the hinges. If the screws don't tighten when turned, and just go around and around, they need new wood to bite into. Remove the screws, hold the door in place, use the now-famous match trick (see page 53) and replace the screws. Loners can manage, but friends as props are mighty nice.

The Electricity System

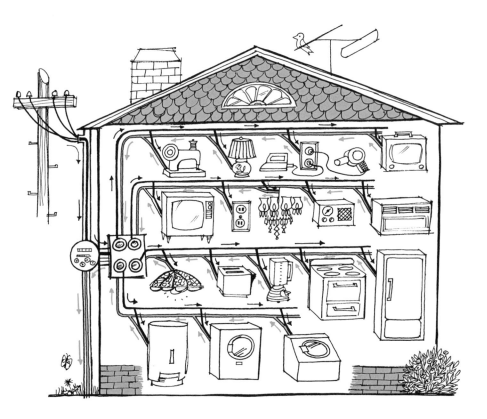

The experts say "treat electricity with respect," or use grand terms like "harnessing energy to bring light into your life." Me, I verge on being terrified, so respect comes easier than fancy phrases. I probably take unnecessary precautions, but I'm happier and less singed.

If you understand what electricity is about—and how home wiring works—it helps you keep terror within reason. Amazingly enough, the basic electrical system isn't wildly complicated.

Your friendly old utility company supplies the main current to your house or apartment. Once the current gets there, it is split up into smaller, workable electrical circuits by your fuse box or circuit breaker.

A black wire carries the current to outlets and switches, and a white wire (sometimes red) takes it back to the source. The black wire is called the "hot" wire, the white the "ground." Electricity has to be a round trip or it won't work. It's always in the wires. Outlets and switches are simply convenient "interruptions" along the way that control your use of electricity.

Before we get into specifics, I should say appliance repair is not *pour moi*. Most heating, cooling and mixing appliances I leave to the professional, if he'll touch them. The servicemen, especially for small appliances, are increasingly ornery about this. Such statements as "Buy a new one," or "It costs more to fix than I dare charge," are common. In all-too-many cases they do have a point. A sky-high proportion of appliances are not really meant to be fixed easily, if at all. You're supposed to just throw them away!

Opening up one of these appliances for repair is Pandora's box indeed. Many are so badly designed inside (to allow for an award-winning design outside) that it's impossible to get at the problem area without special tools and/or hours of finagling. Even if you figure out what's wrong and what part you need to fix it, you often can't find it or get someone to sell the part to you. If you stagger through all of this (I have, a few times), you may still be haunted that some minuscule part is not where it should be.

Big warning! Water likes to conduct electricity like John Philip Sousa liked to conduct bands. Electricity goes for anything wet, even damp versions of feet, hands, floors, walls, rags and sponges. You name it. Electricity's attraction for metal should go without saying. But I'll say it: you'd be horrified how many women use a fork to fish toast out of a hooked-in toaster. The results can be Fourth-of-Julyish.

Big rule! When doing any electrical work in any household area, turn off its current supply at the fuse box or circuit breaker. For plug-in gadgets—appliances, lamps, whatever—always unplug before starting to work.

But first! Where is your *fuse box* or *circuit breaker?* Do you know what they look like? To find one or the other, look on the walls for a small metal door that's usually either painted closed so it won't open, or painted open so it won't close. In an apartment it can be anywhere, usually inconvenient. In a house, it's almost always in the basement. Behind its door a fuse box looks like this,

while a circuit breaker looks like this.

The purpose of both is the same. They split up the main current, as I said before, and protect the wiring system from a dangerous overload of current which could overheat and cause a fire. When overloading occurs (because of a short circuit in an appliance or more often too many things operating on the same line which draws more current than the line should handle), the fuse "blows" or the circuit breaker flips its switch to stop current from flowing into the overloaded area.

Fuses screw into sockets much like plain old light bulbs. They have a little window through which you can see a metal tab. When the circuit is overloaded, this tab "melts,"

breaking the round trip, or circuit,
which then cuts off the electricity to
that area. You can usually spot the
burned out fuse fairly easily, unless, of course, it controls the lights
where the fuse box is.

Naturally, this is almost always the case, so have a flashlight
handy. *Always* have extra fuses on hand. (I must say fuses are
ecumenical. They are determined to blow on Thanksgiving, Rosh
Hashannah and Christmas.) Ideally, although you probably won't,
you should label what each fuse controls. It only takes a couple
of minutes and saves a lot of stumbling and fumbling when dark-
ness strikes. To do it, station a friend on the premises while you
loosen the fuses one at a time. He can tell you what goes out or
off.

Before removing the fuse, pull the main switch if possible. If
not, carefully unscrew the fuse with your fingertips, touching only
the outer edge. Replace the new fuse in the same gingerly fashion
without touching the other parts of the panel or box.

The circuit breaker is a newer
breed, a lot less trouble and a lot
safer. You can't monkey with it even
if you're tempted (see page 61).
When an overload occurs, the
switch involved flips to the "off" position. This is easy to locate because
it's noticeably different from the
line-up of the other switches.

Needless to say, it doesn't make sense to replace a fuse or flip back
the switch before you find out what caused the problem. Since
fuses are very stubborn about protecting you, they'll just blow
again. Most likely, you've turned on one too many heating appliances at the same time.

Picture an all-too-typical Sunday morning with the electric
coffeepot, electric frypan and toaster, with the steam iron on the
sidelines heating to press the dress you've sat in once too often.
Down goes the toast—and poppo!—out go the lights and appli-

ances. Disconnect something, then change the fuse or flip the switch.

Air conditioners, refrigerators and all things with motors can also give you problems. If the lights dim ever so slightly or your TV picture narrows a bit when your refrigerator, for instance, comes on, you're close to the electrical edge. Don't push your luck by adding to the load of that circuit. In fact, change the appliances around to reduce the load if you can.

If you have one fuse that continually blows and some not-so-smart apple suggests putting a penny or a piece of foil behind the fuse so it won't blow—don't do it! Another snappy suggestion you may hear is to get a larger amp* fuse . . . don't do that either!

The fuse and circuit breaker stand between you and an electrical fire. These fires can be nasty ones because they can start in the wall, not necessarily out where you can see them. Better to be bored or mad at changing a fuse or flipping a switch than to burn up Valhalla.

Extensions, Baseboard and Cord.
Practically never in our electrified civilization are there enough outlets for all the appliances, nor are they in the right places. The temptation to buy still another extension cord should be resisted if your floor already looks like spaghetti. Instead, look for a "permanent" type of extension with plug, wire and outlet that can be safely attached to the baseboard or wall. You can either buy this setup as a unit or as separate components and assemble them yourself (see page 64). The latter often works better because

---

* Amp stands for ampere, which is the measure of the amount of electricity that particular line is designed to carry. Most ordinary circuits call for 15-, maybe 20-amp fuses; if you jump to 30 you're asking for trouble.

you are not restricted to standard lengths of cord.

There are terribly involved figurings with volts, amps and watts (for good reason) to guide you in buying the right, adequate extension cord for different uses. I found my mind boggled with the mathematics, and the following served me well. Buy an extension cord like the cord you want to extend. For instance, the thicker cords for appliances and tools are that way because they're needed to carry the heavier power loads. The extension cord should be the same type. Comparing your toaster cord with a lamp cord will give you the idea. If you're dealing with damp areas, be sure the cord is waterproof and the plug is sealed against water.

Be sure to get a good quality. Five-and-dime-store stuff is OK for short distances and lamps, but shouldn't be counted on for much else. Any cord you buy should carry a UL tag (Underwriters Laboratories). It's the standard seal of approval for good, safe electrical supplies. Short-changing can only lead to short-circuiting.

Fluorescent Lights. This is tube territory, not bulb. Despite your fears, the tubes are easy to change. The tube is not screwed in, but fits into

end arms (sockets) of the holding
unit and locks into place with a
quarter turn. The only caution is
the word turn. Don't twist. Glass
doesn't do that at all well.

To replace a blinky or burned-out
tube (although you may never have
to, they seem to last for years), remove it with a quarter turn. Take
the tube to the electrical or hardware store to find one like it. If the
new tube still blinks, chances are
the "starter" is faulty. This usually
is located in the holding unit, behind or under the tube. Then again,
it may be on the outside. Discourag-
ing, isn't it?

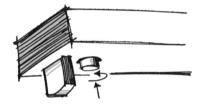

The starter can be removed by
pressing in and giving about a half
turn. To replace the starter almost
always means a trip to the electrical
supply store.

The round type of fluorescent
ceiling fixture is held by spring supports. Again, gently does it. Pull it
free of the springs and then disconnect.

If you want to venture into the
cosmetic advantages of fluorescents
to your home, see page 111.

LAMPS

Four things can go wrong with a lamp, whether it hangs from
the wall, sets on a table or stands on the floor—the bulb, the cord,
the plug, the switch. Start with the bulb because it's easy and also
it burns out far too fast. Next check the cord for breaks or wear

spots, particularly where it enters the lamp base or the plug. Jiggle the cord. If the light flickers, it's either a short circuit inside the cord or a loose connection in the plug (see page 66). The switch is the most complicated and the least likely to go, so save that for last. Actually, the following will discuss cords, plugs and switches, applicable to lamps or otherwise, new or replacement.

Cords. Whether you're putting a new cord on a plug and/or switch or working with an existing cord, here's the basic procedure to follow. Since most cords today already have the wires divided into the molded channels (electricity's "round trip," remember?), take your razor knife and cut through the middle of these channels a distance of about 2". Then about 1" in from the now separated ends, cut *around* each one. Don't get heavy-handed and cut through the fine wires inside. Pull the cut parts off, leaving the wires exposed. If the cord is a "one piece" construction, the individual channels are inside and do not show. For this type, cut around the outside and pull off (unravel if it's fabric-covered) the overall outside insulation, then remove the inside insulation on the individual wires, again about 1" in. For either type of cord, when you have each set of fine wires bared (they'll look frayed), twist each bunch so that you have a wire instead of lots of little wires. From this point, you tackle the individual problem.

There are times when, instead of getting into a complicated rewiring of a whole thing, like a six-way lamp, you can fix a minor outside "break" in the cord by splicing. The dictionary definition of *splicing:* to join together or unite by the interweaving of strands. My advice is, if you don't have to splice, don't. Instead of repairing a rupture in the cord, replace it whenever feasible. Perhaps I prefer replacement because I've never been noted for my bandaging or taping abilities—lumpy, you know. But if you have to splice, there are almost as many variations as there are Boy Scout knots. I'm no good at tying knots, either. I'm still at the stage of taking a string and doing "here's a tree, here's the rabbit's hole, the rabbit runs around the tree and down the hole." In my amateur way, I guess I use what the whizzes call the Western Union splice. Without knowing the terminology, I just spliced that way and it worked. Here's how to go about it.

Cut through each channel of wire at a different place, about an inch or so apart. This keeps the end result from being too lumpy. Strip the insulation from the two sets of wires. Cross the two ends in each channel of each set and wind them back around themselves. Then tape the wounds with electrical tape, thusly, first separately, then together.

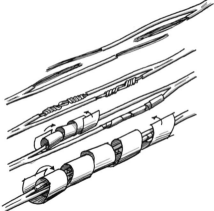

Plugs. If the existing plug is molded plastic or rubber, simply cut it from the cord with scissors or wire clippers. You'll have to throw it away because there's no way to get inside it to reconnect the cord. If the plug is the screw variety, you only need to unscrew the wires (see below). Unplug it first unless you want a free trip across the room. If you want to shorten the cord, now's the time to do it.

The types of plugs available and possible for you to use in replacing the defective one are the "screw" and the "clamp."

The *screw* type is the more common and also the only kind you should or can use for heavier cords. First, strip the wires as described before under Cords. To wire the screw plug, pull a section of the cord through from the bottom of the plug and tie what's called an Underwriter's knot. This knot should only involve the parts of the wire that are still insulated, so strip the wires after you tie the knot. It's hopeless to explain in words, so I'll resort to the only Latin I can remember: *Discipuli picturum spectate* (Pupils, look at the picture). Otherwise you're asking for pure disaster. This knot helps keep the wires in place even if you have the bad habit of yanking the cord out of an outlet, or two left feet that keep tripping over cords.

When you've tied the knot, pull the cord back through until the knot snuggles in between the prongs. Loosen the screws at the base of each prong on the plug face. Then take each wire bunch clockwise around the prong and curl it, again clockwise, under the screw.

Tighten both screws, making sure the wires stay tucked in as much as possible. I say "clockwise" because that's the way screws tighten, so this allows them to work with the wires, not against. Put the

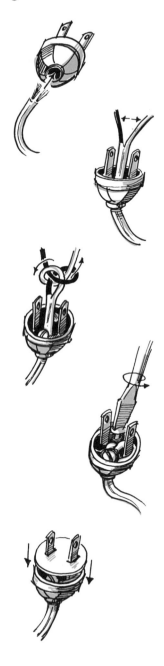

insulating plate over the prongs, flat to the face and plug in.

The *clamp* type has been designed so that it does not require cord stripping or screws to hold the wires. The principle is the use of pressure to force the two metal points of the clamp through the insulation to make contact with the inside wires.

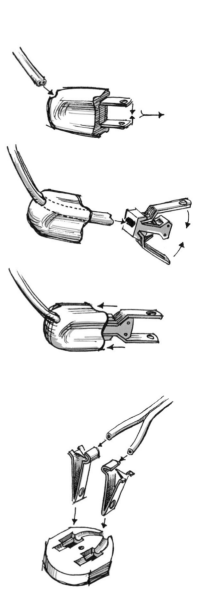

There is a variety of clamp-type plugs. With one you have a plug "core" which contains prongs and the outer shell. You feed the cord through the shell into the core. The prongs should be open or "butterflied" to allow the cord to go in completely. You then close the prongs and insert the core into the shell. Some of these clamp plugs have a locking device on the shell which holds the cord in place instead of simply relying on a close fit to hold the core and shell together.

The flat clamp plug is great for kitchen counters and tight spots. It does require that you separate the channels of the cord. The metal points are forced through the cord when you screw the back onto the face.

There are two problems which have occurred with clamp plugs. More often than not, the little metal points don't quite bite through the cord insulation. If the light, or whatever, doesn't work, unplug and unassemble the plug. Take your trusty ice pick or end of a scissors blade and open up the little punctures in the wires made by the points. Don't go too big, but you should be able to see a glint of copper wire.

The second problem is that the cord may pull out of the clamp plug. If this happens, don't touch any part of the plug remaining in the socket. Cut off the power to that outlet. Remove the remains, and depending on damage done, either reassemble or replace.

Switches. There are three kinds of switches—lamp, midwire and wall—that I can help you do something about. I stay away from those mixed up with appliances, as I said before.

LAMP SWITCH. If either the in-and-out or knob-turn type of switch start to slip and lose their definitive action, you need a new switch. Here's what a working switch looks like when it's pulled apart.

The bottom part of the switch has nothing that can go wrong with it and most new switches will fit into it. So don't touch. It's often what holds the rest of the lamp together. To ensure a proper fit, take the outer part, or shell, of the switch with you to the hardware or electric supply store for one like it.

Understand, you'll have to buy the whole unit but you may save yourself some work.

To get the old switch unit off, unplug the lamp, remove shade and bulb; press right above the bottom part (sometimes the word "press" is stamped on the shell to show you where) and pull apart. I've not always had it that easy and have been known to resort to pliers and curses to get the parts apart. Remove the cardboard insulator tube and loosen the two screws that hold the wires. You're now ready to install the new switch.

Take the new switch apart as you did the old. Attach the wires, put the insulator collar on, put the shell on and then put the entire unit back into the bottom section of the switch. This is the point where and how you replace the cord if need be. Use the desired length of channeled cord and strip as described on page 64. To make it easy to feed the new cord through the middle of the lamp, tie a long piece of string (longer than the lamp is high) to the old cord. Pull the old cord out through the bottom, and hang on to the string so it doesn't go through too. Untie the old cord. Then tie the new cord to the string and pull it back up

through the lamp. Proceed with wiring, and assemble.

MIDWIRE SWITCH. Many hanging wall lamps and more and more table lamps have a switch on the wire instead of on the lamp itself. At some point it may go on the fritz. It's usually small and attractive, but not tough enough to stand the wear and tear of constant use. Resist getting its twin as a replacement and buy a larger, uglier, stronger one. Unplug the lamp and take off the old switch by removing the little snap bands or screws which hold the switch together. Open up the new switch by removing the two screws (or nuts and bolts) on the switch that hold it together. Fit the uncut continuous channel of the lamp cord in the designated channel of the switch. Then take the cut parts of the cord and attach as you would for a plug —clockwise and all that! (See page 66.)

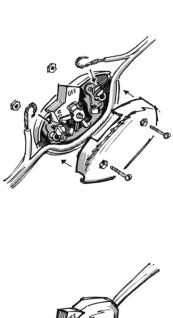

If you want to put a midwire switch on a cord where there hasn't been one, pick your spot on the wire. For a channeled cord, separate the channels and cut completely through one of them. Strip bare the cut wire and do as described for the replacing of a faulty midwire switch. If the cord is not a divided-channel type, cut

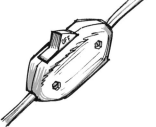

out a section of the outer insulation
(see page 64). Then separate the
wires, cut and strip only the one
you'll hook to the screws, and proceed.

WALL SWITCH. Although this may
seem to be the scariest because
you're dealing with the basic wiring of the house or apartment (and
that's hot stuff), it really is quite
simple. In effect, you "unplug" the
switch by pulling the appropriate
fuse or circuit breaker. Even if
you've labeled the circuits as
suggested on page 60, turn the
switch on first to make sure that
whatever it controls goes out or off.
It's mind-relieving to know it's
definitely OK to go ahead. Chances
are you'll need a flashlight. Remove the outside plate by undoing
the screw or screws. Now you'll
see the switch itself.

Take out the top and bottom
screws to free the switch so that
you can pull it out to get to the
wires. Here, possibly for the first
time, you'll meet the white wire
and the black wires. Remember
them (page 58)? As I said, these
are the mainstays of all home wiring. The black wire is the "hot"
one. If you run into extra wires
(usually red), this is because your
switch does more than simply turn
one thing on and off. For instance,

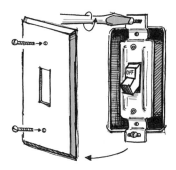

whatever you turn on here you can turn off at some other place, with another switch. Note where the extra wire or wires hook on to the switch, and put them back the same way on the new switch. In fact, note the same with the white and the black, too. Even if the existing wiring arrangement looks nutty to you, it's best to follow it. If you have any doubts about the replacement switch you need, take the old switch to the hardware or electrical supply store, with a note of where (and what color) the wires connect to it. Your new switch can be a plain replacement, or you can change to a mercury (the quiet model) or a dimmer switch. Because dimmers are for lights only, do not try to use them where the switch also controls an outlet that might be used for appliances.

Hook the black wire(s) to the dark brassy-looking side of the new switch, and the white wire(s) to the light silvery side of it. Clockwise with the wires, please. Tighten the screws over the wires and fold the extra wire behind the switch, then press switch, wires and all back into the hole. Replace the top and bottom screws, then the cover plate. If for any reason you

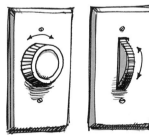

get mixed up or both wires are black, don't worry. Nothing drastic happens. The switch just won't work. Simply undo the switch as before and change the wires. Don't forget to turn the power off again.

Wall Outlets. These are what you plug everything into. I'm not suggesting that you create new ones. Leave that to the professional electrician or improvise with "permanent-type" extension (see page 61). To replace a faulty outlet, go about the wiring business as you did for the wall switch. Turn off the power and remove the outside plate and undo the inside holding screws. Here you're more likely to run into extra wires. If this is the case, you'll find two whites and two blacks, or sometimes a red if the wall outlet is controlled by a wall switch. Connect them as they were on the old outlet.

A marvelous offshoot of the outlet is a multiple-plug version that can easily be installed on top of existing, working, two-plug outlets. Remove the plate and screw the new version into place. If you go mad and plug in every appliance you own, it'll mean a trip to the fuse box, of course.

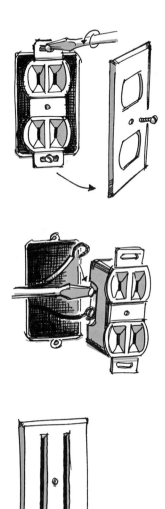

❊ ❊ ❊

Floors, Refinishing Wood. Your floors look terrible and you want them clean and shiny. Yes, Virginia, you can rent a real floor sander. Don't you dare! First, you won't be able to lift, move or budge the monster (it weighs a small ton) unless it's turned on. When it is turned on, it takes off like a runaway horse. If your floors really need sanding and you're a renter, your land-lord *should* have the job done but don't count on it. Definitely ask that this be done before you move in. If the floors are yours, hire a professional service.

However, you can sand bad spots and worn areas with a rented electric hand sander. You'll be able to manage this equip-ment, but then the problem is that the ex-badspot will prob-ably become the best part of the floor and won't match the rest.

With floors, prevention truly is better than the cure. Over-protect the busy traffic areas with extra and frequent coats of wax.

If you have to remove an accumulation of wax, there is a nonheralded product called "Mex" that does an absolutely phenomenal job. It's available at most hardware stores.

If the floor finish isn't too bad, often a good cleaner/wax used with fine steel wool will bring it back up to snuff. My mother tells me the orange net onion bags are better scrubbers than steel wool.

Furniture, Minor Repairs. For a stain or scratch, my favorite solution is to move an ashtray or objet d'art over it and hope only the snoops will notice.

However, some villains really do need at least a college try to make them less obvious if not totally disappear. If the injured surface is solid wood, experiment away. Veneer (more common) is touchier. After all, it's just a thin layer of wood on wood—so gently does it. There are touch-up and filler kits on sale which are pretty good but don't expect the perfection they promise. In the hands of a furniture refinisher you'd get the acclaimed results, but of course if you're a furniture refinisher you wouldn't need the kit. And so it goes. If you feel adventurous, try some of these home-grown cures.

VILLAIN #1—The ubiquitous glass-ring mark. Although it may not be banished totally, you can make a pretty good stab at it by following this route. Take fine, fine steel wool, coated lightly with a cleaner/polisher liquid wax and rub the wood firmly and evenly. Don't dig. Keep at it, adding wax as you need. This remedy really does correct most of the cases, especially if you don't sight along the surface at eye level toward the light. If you really have a white, white ring on dark woods, take a cotton swab dipped in iodine, appropriately colored shoe polish or artist's oil paint thinned with turpentine, or paste made out of instant coffee and water. For lighter woods, dilute the above to lighten the color to match. In all cases, allow the "stain" to dry then wax over the whole surface after giving the treatment time to sit. If wood is blond, the fine-steel-wool–wax treatment alone should work. Another home remedy for removing water marks is sprinkling the stain with salt and rubbing with a cloth dipped in olive oil.

VILLAIN #2—Scratches. These can be disguised by the same camouflage techniques as for Villain #1, unless you're dealing with a Grand Canyon. Then either use one of the commercial fillers or an ordinary coloring crayon closest to the color of the wood. If it really is a big, deep scratch, try to dig away a little at the bottom of the scratch to give you a wider base with an overhang on the surface. This tends to hold the filler in place.

VILLAIN #3—Burns. Cigarette-burn scar tissue can be scraped away carefully with a paring knife first; then you can use either or both of the previous treatments. A bad burn is tough to cover because the width makes it hard to get an even, solid fill. Settle for a color match or figure out an alternate approach such as covering the tabletop with marble, tile, cork or self-adhesive plastic sheet. With the last, fill the burn in evenly with spackle or wood filler first so the scar indentations don't show through.

NON-WOOD VILLAINS. I'm not a clear-plastic admirer, at least of big pieces like coffee tables and storage cubes. They just seem cold and unforgiving to me, but "Everyone to his own taste." Anyway, Lucite lovers tell me scratches are a real bane. They also recommend toothpaste to remove the most frequent, lesser scratches. It sounds right, and I don't think you'd have to bother whether the toothpaste contains fluoride or not.

A deep burn in a carpet can become a no-show by scratching away the charred bits with your fingernail or a table knife. Then collect some of the fuzz of the carpet from your vacuum-cleaner brush or scratch fuzz from an obscure spot of the carpet. Put glue along the bottom of the burn mark and press in the fuzz.

Furniture, Outdoor. The joys of a terrace are not undiluted (or is it unpolluted?), particularly in dirty old cities. If you have a terrace, the only sane, not wildly expensive choice is a combination aluminum and plastic furniture. It may not be as posh as curlicue wrought iron (iron, being iron, painted or not, will rust) but it can stay outside summer and *winter* (storage space being what it is) and hold its own.

Although carefree is the adjective most often used to describe this furniture, a little care can keep you way ahead in the dirt game. Wax all metal surfaces with good paste wax. A couple of coats will do for a start. Repeat once or twice during the season, especially if you scrubbed the rest of the chair with a strong detergent, to keep the metal from pitting. If some pitting has occurred, use a steel-wool soap pad to get the bumps and scale off, rinse and then wax as before. Incidentally, the wax treatment won't hurt the fancier wrought-iron furniture and will help it resist rust. However, check out spray wax for this job. Although it doesn't give as heavy a wax coating, it can get into all those nooks and crannies.

If your furniture has plastic-tape backs and seats that need replacing, you can find suitable kits or tape by the yard at most department and some hardware stores. Before you undo the old, notice how it's put together in case the directions are obscure or you're working with just the tape.

Moving In/Moving Out

MOVING IN. In apartments, first things first. If you can find the superintendent, tip (bribe) him. If nothing else, this down-payment tells him you understand the ledger of life.

Do your damnedest to get into the apartment (not to live) before the telephone man and the painters do. Be sure to take a putty knife and small screwdriver with you. If you plan to have the phone moved (or there are leftover wires from other installations), pull all the wires free of the baseboards. Either cut them off or curl them up near the entry box. If you're contemplating installing your own extension phone—save the cord. Ninety percent of the time the phone company won't remove old wires and you can bet the painters won't. They just paint right over anything that doesn't move. Proof of this is in some older buildings where you'll find literally layers of wires. So pull them free. This tidies up the baseboard and gets rid of dirt catchers, too. Use the putty knife to even off the mountains and valleys of dried paint that have accumulated behind the obsolete wires. The screwdriver can pry out old wire staples and remove any electric switch or outlet plates that you don't want painted.

Check out the faucets for drips; look for smoke marks on the wall if there's a fireplace; turn on the stove burners, check out the oven and refrigerator. Big item—flush the john a couple of times. People often use it as a catch-all and throw the weirdest things down it when they clean out the medicine cabinet. Also, if the painters and/or plasterers have been around, their contributions to the plumbing of Spackle and the like can cause interesting problems.

The point is that the time to get trouble fixed (if ever) is *before* you move in, while the money still burns brightly in the super's mind.

Don't forget to zero in on the curtain/drapery rods, and if they're at all usable, be adamant about their staying. Insist on the Venetian blinds being cleaned so you don't have to do a nudie act for the neighbors.

You used to be able to insist on floors being sanded and waxed. These days, however, if they're halfway decent, you'll have a hard time getting them refinished.

Another good thing to do beforehand or even on the actual moving day, if you're being commercially moved, is to cover kitchen and closet shelves and line drawers. You can buy lengths of a sticky-backed plastic that comes in a splendid variety of colors and designs. Besides being pretty, it's practical and makes later clean-ups a breeze. For the how-to of this, see page 123.

Before putting sticky-backed plastic down or things away, it's a good idea to spray an insecticide in the closets, cupboards and on baseboards to evict any leftover tenants like moths, silverfish and cockroaches. The last two usually depart with the painting. They hate the paint and change residence just to get away from it all. That's a bit of info to remember after you're in and *you* get a new neighbor. You may get more than that.

Almost immediately establish your credit for check-cashing privileges at a nearby store. Possibilities are the supermarkets and liquor stores, but somehow the liquor dealers are much nicer about it. When the state runs the liquor store, the latter obviously can't be done. But in civilized society, banks being a bit overly so, these local stores are a nighttime and Saturday godsend. If you know anybody who can vouch for you, that speeds things up. Barring that, throw a housewarming party and pay for the party by check. That will get your credit started. By the bye, be sure the check won't bounce.

If it's raining on moving-in day—doesn't it always—it's worth a sprint to the dime store to buy a few yards of plastic runner. The wear, dirt and tear this saves on floors and rugs, if they're down, is blessed.

MOVING OUT. The M.O. here is to cover your sins and take along what belongs to you. About the sins—mostly they're the holes caused by Mollys, shields, anchors, nails and picture hangers. The cover-up is particularly worthwhile—toward getting your deposit back—if you've done big things like hanging bookshelves on the wall.

Some people say they would rather not bother with or risk adding individual decorating or convenience touches in a rental. But when it's so easy to restore the status quo if necessary, it seems to me two or three years is a long time to exist like a monk.

In one of the over-closeted apartments I had, I converted one of the living-room closets into a bar. I stashed away the clothes rod and shelf lumber in another closet, and then simply put it back together before I moved. A half-hour's rebuild allowed me three years' worth of a kitchen free of the glasses, accouterments and helpful guests.

Here are some suggestions to undo all those things you have done:

For Mollys and their cousins, shields and anchors, take a sturdy, big-headed nail or screw, put the head on the end of the fastener that shows and hammer until it moves below the wall surface. Repeat this until every one is pounded into the wall. Pull out picture hangers and nails and anything that wasn't in the wall when you arrived. Don't worry if some of the plaster flakes off. Get the putty knife and spackle over all the holes and scars.

Any of the good-quality vinyl-coated fabric wall coverings and some wallpapers can be removed by grabbing a corner and pulling. You should wash the wall down afterward to get rid of the dried glue and roughness. If you don't, the painters who follow will paint right over it, and that's not fair to the next tenants. Incidentally, if you see the tenants, check if they want the covering left. The landlord can't object and you save yourself some work.

If you can swing it, consider hiring a commercial mover. On the negative side, the prices are outrageous, and the workers, once the best, are going the way of all flesh—doing less for more. But guess where they learned it? The company will tell you the government sets the rates. True, but unless someone's gotten altruistic, the price the movers give you is the maximum rate they are allowed to charge, not the minimum they could. Not surprisingly, estimates from the larger companies are as alike as peas in a pod. However, you may be able to get a better deal with a smaller, local mover. Check carefully though and try to get a recommendation from someone who has used them.

On the positive side, the moving companies supply (for a price) boxes and barrels that are the right size and strength for your possessions. Unless you're rich or somebody else is paying for the move, forgo the packers. You can do it yourself easily.

Some good rules to follow are: Put heavy items on the bottom and build around and up from there. Try not to combine breakable items (china and glass) with non-shock-absorbing, nonbreakable ones (iron skillets, appliances). Overdo the paper as cushioning and wrapping around, over, between and under. Save your newspapers for weeks ahead—you'll need them all.

An X-ray of a typical packed barrel might be:

Crunch up newspaper to create a springy bed for items to rest on. Use paper like this along the sides, bottom, top and whenever you finish off a layer.

To wrap small breakables, single sheets of a regular newspaper or a double of a tabloid will provide enough cushioning without getting too unwieldy.

To wrap larger items, use two or three double sheets of regular-sized newspaper.

Snug-fitting and well-cushioned is the word. The wrapping will go faster if you work on a table. Open up flat a pile of newspapers and work your way from the top down.

Seal the boxes with brown sticky paper tape. Get it good and wet by seesawing it under running cold water. Drain and tape. List the contents of the box on the outside with a flow pen or a big crayon. You'd be surprised how fast you forget what's where. Cataloging can save clutter and time on the other end.

If you do move yourself, see your (hopefully) friendly grocery or liquor-store man. The latter has boxes which, even though they're small, are designed to carry weight. When you realize one twin sheet weighs two pounds, you can see why regular unreinforced cartons can cause side-splitting crises when you least need them.

Always keep one box around for last-moment collections and second thoughts. On the other end of the move, it will seem like a grab bag, but invaluable nevertheless. Once at my place, last in and first out somehow or other was an iron frypan wrapped in a black lace slip.

Plumbing

HOW TO TURN OFF THE WATER

This knowledge is vital not only for doing some minor pipe work but in case the toilet's cup runneth over. Preferably, do a "better safe than sorry" bit and find where any or all of these cut-offs are soon after moving in. Apartments, especially old ones, are something else again. Some just blissfully ignore the fixture cut-off valves. You might as well do the same and pray a little. If disaster strikes, run for the super and hope he's around to turn off the water. Mercifully, there is usually a cut-off valve (a wheel-looking thing or two if there is hot and cold water) on the pipe leading to each plumbing fixture. If the floods come, dive for the valve (it's usually near the floor) and turn it clockwise until it and the water stop. In newer apartments, where the bathroom backs up to the kitchen, you'll sometimes find the cut-off valves for the bathroom under the kitchen sink. If you don't have individual cut-off valves (urk!) run, don't walk, to the basement or utility room instead. There's where the main cut-off valve should be. It's usually stolidly sitting near the water meter. Clockwise is the action here, too.

Drains, Clogged. It's mostly what you put down a drain, accidentally or not, that clogs it up or slows it down. In the kitchen you can almost bet on grease, either all by itself or with little treasures caught around the edges. And despite persistent advice to the contrary, coffee grounds are bad news. In bathroom sinks or tubs, hair and suds' curd are usually the culprits. In almost all cases, any of the commercial drain cleaners will do the trick. Treat them with respect. The same chemical action that eats its way through the drain block can do the same to you. Don't use it at all if water is standing and not even draining slowly. More and more cleaners claim it doesn't matter, but I still wouldn't chance it. With some, the water sets off the chemical action of the cleaner. If this happens outside the drain, not inside where the stoppage is—and doesn't work—you could have a real problem and a touchy job to get rid of the highly caustic solution (see page 31). With the other cleaners, you've got the same problem—if they don't work. Do it right and be on the safe side.

The best bet is to use a cup or your turkey baster to remove the standing water, first. In kitchen sinks, remove the drain basket. Elsewhere, take out the plug for the drain if you can.

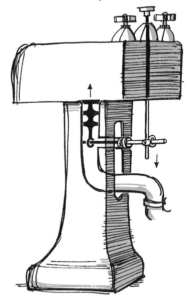

For bathroom basins, usually the plug comes out with a simple turning and lifting action. If the plug is attached from the outside, look under the backside of the basin. You'll see two rods held together by a nut and bolt. In most cases you can disconnect the rods where they join by unscrewing the bolt. You'll then be able to lift the plug out.

If you simply can't get the plug out, work around it carefully. Use the drain cleaner, following directions explicitly—they are not kidding!

If the drain is clogged, remove the water, plug or basket and get out the "plumber's helper" (page 9). Put it over the opening and work it up and down several times. If there's an overflow hole plug it with a rag. It helps increase the suction action of the "helper." Don't be discouraged if great results don't happen right off. Keep at it. Don't expect to see the evidence. You're trying to break up the mass down inside the pipe. When even a little drainage is noted, switch to a chemical cleaner and you should be on your way to free-flowing plumbing. If *no* drainage is noted, keep your little hands off the cleaner and remove the clean-out plug in the pipe itself.

This plug is the nutty-looking part that's at the bottom of the bend (gooseneck) in the pipe. Put a bucket under it first, then, with pliers or a wrench, loosen and remove it. Fish around inside the pipe as best you can with a straightened-out coat hanger. With luck you'll break up the blockage enough to get some water through. Turn on a faucet to see if the water drains. That's one reason for the bucket. Poke around some more with the coat hanger and you may dislodge all of the blockage. If you don't, replace the plug and use the chemical cleaner. It may take a couple of doses but it's safe to use if the water is draining.

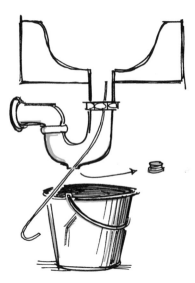

If all this fails, the stoppage may be some place else, or you've put a real no-no down the drain. There are further measures you could take, but my advice is, don't. You're in deep enough already. Replace the plug, close up your tool kit and retreat with as much grace as you can manage to call the super or the plumber. Let him be responsible.

Faucets. There are so many versions of these and probably no picture will match yours, but here are some samples anyway:

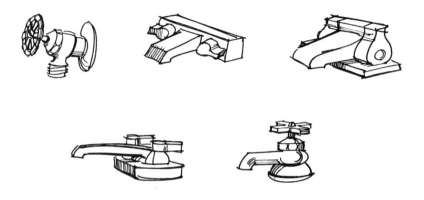

Be of good cheer. The insides of faucets, no matter how fancy the façade, are essentially the same. To control the water, there is a little water-tight plug (washer) that seals the hole from whence springeth the water. When you turn on the water you "unplug" the hole, when you turn off the water you "plug" the hole.

To keep water from coming up through the small space where the stem meets the handle (instead of out of the hole it's supposed to) there's a seal called a packing nut.

Some of the newer faucets have inside designs that are much simpler and longer-lived. Virtually nothing goes wrong with them. If something does, the insides can be replaced with a unit, complete with specific directions. You can buy this at a plumbing supply house or some hardware stores. Take an old bath towel and lay it in the basin or sink.

This averts small disasters caused by your dropsies, such as parts going down the drain or chips in the porcelain if a tool slips or falls.

To fix what ails most faucets you have to get the handle off first. The big trick with some is to find the screw or nut that keeps the handle in place. Keep looking. It's there someplace. Most times it's disguised as the H or C. These usually will either snap out or unscrew. Turn off the water if you haven't already.

Note the angle of the handle in the "off" position so you can put it back in the same place when finished. To get the handle off, if you're involved with a chrome nut, cover either that or the pliers (wrench, depending on size) with tape so that the teeth won't munch on the finish. Remove the screw on the handle and work the handle free of the stem. The handle may be stubborn. If so, gently "force" it off with a screwdriver or move it back and forth with your hands. This stem has a knurled base which keeps the handle from slipping and which positions it properly.*

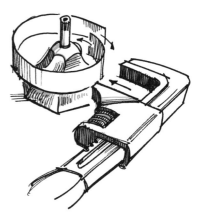

* If your faucets are supposed to look like ⟨img⟩ but instead assume this rakish angle ⟨img⟩ , you can often get them back on the beam by simply pulling off handle and reseating it to match the other.

LEAKY FAUCET. *If the problem is drip, drip, drip* and it's driving you nuts, look to the washer. Since you may not know what kind of washer is in there, buy an inexpensive assortment package at the five-and-ten, hardware store or supermarket. Get this before you begin your repairs.

Now loosen and remove the packing nut, then the stem. Keep the parts in order so you don't add complications when reassembling.

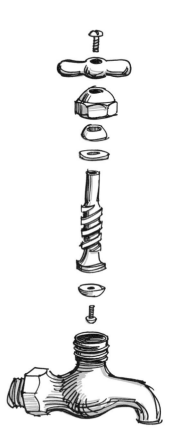

You'll find a screw in the bottom of the stem. If the screw gives you trouble, pry out the washer from around it and then use pliers to remove the screw. If it's corroded or defective, replace the screw with a new brass one. Pick out a new washer that is the exact size and shape as the old and put it on with the rounded side down (if there is a rounded side. Some washers are flat).

Through all this you may have problems with loosening and replacing the parts. I did and so do most amateurs afraid of breaking things. Patience is the password. Get mad if that makes you determined; don't if you throw things. Keep at it, you'll win. After you finish, if the faucet is too tight, loosen the packing nut slightly or put a drop or so of silicone coater on the stem.

If water wells up from inside the faucet and leaks out around the handle when you turn it on, the

packing nut's the culprit. If tightening the nut doesn't help, the packing inside is shot. Remove the nut
as before. Inside the nut there's
usually some sort of gummy packing material or a washer—maybe
both. Get out the ice pick and dig
it/them out. Take the remains and
the nut between thumb and fore-
finger to the hardware store and get
the same ilk. Repack the nut and
reassemble the faucet.

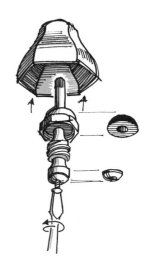

Bathtub and shower faucets are
identical to those in the sink. However, they are more difficult to fix,
since the wall tile may make getting to the environs a problem.
Some bright soul has designed a
special socket wrench (a must) for
that job. Any self-respecting hardware store or plumbing supply department should have one.

Leaky Pipes. If one of the lead-in pipes to any of the fixtures
springs a pinhole leak, your finger in the dike can be epoxy
cement. It promises to seal even wet surfaces and it does fairly
well. However, if you can turn off the water, the cement will work
easier and faster, because it doesn't have to battle water pressure.
This will not work on a real blow-out. When this happens, turn
off the water and call for professional help.

Toilets. "Toilet tank" is more like it. The works are a true "ankle-
bone connected to the legbone, legbone connected to the kneebone, kneebone connected to the thighbone" thing. There are
newer, considerably less "Rube Goldberg" arrangements, but if
your toilet is new, chances are you won't have to do anything
with it. So, on to the old.

There's the handle,   which

moves

the

trip

arm

which pulls up the
lift wire which

pulls up the lift
wire
which

pulls up the flush
ball

and the water goes
out of the tank
to flush the toilet.

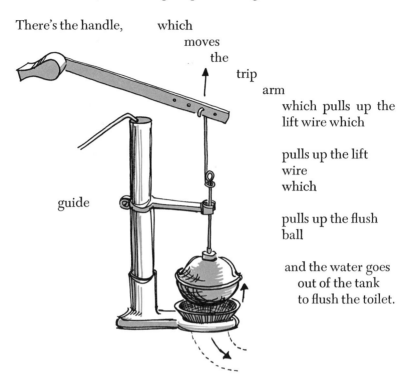

guide

As that happens, there's another scene of action going on. When
the water leaves the tank

the tank float drops

(it has nothing to float on)

and opens the inlet valve

and

here

to fill

the bowl

and water
comes in

here
to fill
the tank

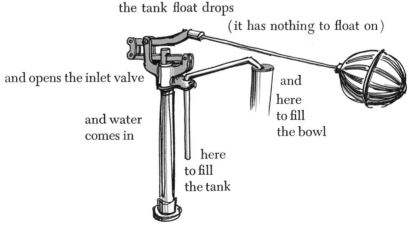

Put them all together and you'll see how the whole works operates and what it actually looks like.

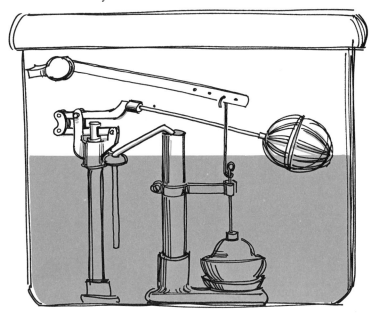

Now you know what should go on—when it doesn't, here are some remedies. For all problems, lift off the top of the tank. If the tank is not filling, the flush ball is not settling properly and not doing its job of closing the water in. Chances are you've been handle-jiggling for weeks. Sometimes the guide has shifted off center and is putting the ball off course. Check that. Usually the fault is with one of the lift wires. Either straighten or bend it, depending on where it's missing. Don't be too drastic with the cure. Hit the handle again and see where the ball plops. Continue fiddling until it zeroes in on the outlet. For this job I leave the water on. It's icy going but rarely takes long and it's easier to check the minute changes.

If there is a chain instead of lift wires, the solution usually is to take up the slack by shortening the chain a link or so. If you find other variations, like a leather strap (positively medieval), shorten that too. In any case, what you're aiming for is a straight-down, on-target drop.

If the ball still doesn't seat well, it may be the seat of the outlet itself. This happens more often in areas where the water is hard or dirty. Turn off the water at the toilet cutoff valve. Remove the ball by holding it in your one hand and unscrewing the lift wire with the other. Clean the seat with steel wool. Turn on the water and try it. Still not so good? Maybe the ball and lift wire have seen better days. You can easily get replacements of either or both at the hardware store.

If the tank is filled but the water continues to run, the inlet valve isn't closing properly. Take the rod that holds the tank float and raise it slightly. If the water stops, bend the rod until the float is at that height when left to its own devices. If that doesn't work, the float is probably water-logged. It should not be an iceberg more under than floating. About half in the water and half out is right. Unscrew the float from the rod and replace with the newer solid-plastic type which should end *that* problem for all time.

When none of these suggestions end the problems, you can figure the works are kaput. Rather than repair it piecemeal, the whole glorious apparatus should be replaced. If you're renting, you may not want to get into this complication and expense. Certainly try to get your landlord to do it. If you get nowhere and just can't stand the Chinese water torture, you can buy a complete kit of the tank insides and readily do the job. Don't forget to turn off the water!

One toilet problem unrelated to the tank is the stopped-up one. No drain cleaners here. The only recourse is the plumber's helper (see page 9). Well, not quite. There's always the plumber himself. But try the helper first. Unless you have put plaster or some other nonsoluble down the toilet, or there's trouble elsewhere, with dedicated effort the dam will bust.

Towel Racks, Soap Dishes, Paper Holders. There are basically two kinds of these fixtures—one where whatever holds them up shows, and one where it doesn't. However, there now is one kind with good quality chrome and construction where the screws are partially hidden. Unfortunately, the easiest of these to put up are also usually of the worst quality. The barest coating of chrome is what you get for your money. If you don't mind the screws showing, fine, but rust and scale will show up on the metal in no time. Try coating the metal parts with clear nail polish or spraying with plastic lacquer before putting the fixture up. They are still selling the kinds of fixtures that go up fast with suction cups or glue. My experience has been that they come down almost as fast. However, the ones that utilize epoxy glue have had some nice things said about them.

For the real, built-in look, combined with a sturdy, solid chrome finish, either in all metal or clear plastic and metal, pay more and get what I call a "hidden" plate fixture.

The principle is this: A metal plate with turned-up edge is screwed into the wall or door. This is the base for a chrome metal piece that goes on over and covers the "hidden" plate and is held in place by tightening a small set screw (see page 13) in the bottom which catches under the turned-up edge. When it's a single plate unit like a glass-and-toothbrush holder, ring towel rack and soap dish, it's easy to install. But it's a bit trickier when you have two plates for each end of a toilet-paper holder or towel bar. Not bad, but getting the two plates in line and the right distance apart needs some exact measuring or one hell of a good eye. I'm not exactly cross-eyed, but I measure.

To get the overall size of the fixture and the right side of the fixture
on the right side and the left on the
left (the downside set screw will
clue you in), assemble the rack on
the floor and measure. By pushing
in against each side, you can pick
up the unit and determine the placement you wish on the wall. When
you get that set, remove the left end
and the middle part, holding the
right end tight where it was. (I'm
only saying "right" in order to make
it easier to keep track of the following directions. It doesn't really
make any difference which end you
begin with.) Mark lightly along the
bottom and side of the right unit.
Naturally you should have a pencil
to do this. You won't, so go get one
and go through the whole routine
again. Chances are your positioning
of the fixture has been pretty close
to where you want it. But it really is
best to measure out the length from
the side mark to be sure you have
the fixture placed properly. Adjust
the side mark if you have to. Take
the right unit and line it flush with
this mark and even with the bottom
mark and draw all the way around.
Try the best you can to be sure the
unit is not off at an angle. You
might as well use your eye here.
Most walls aren't straight anyway,

so measuring from the corner rarely
helps. Remove the unit and find one
of the plates. If it isn't turned up on
all sides, be sure to get one turned-
up edge aimed downward. Center
the plate within the penciled area
and mark where the screws go. If
you are working on wood, proceed
with the screw department. If it's
plaster, you'll need to use fiber
plugs (page 16) and screw into
those.

If you're putting up any of the fixtures (even the single plate)
on a hollow door, try the screws alone. You never know—sometimes they hold, sometimes not. After a time, if they pull out, use
⅜" or small neoprene Mollys.

After you get the plate up, install the unit by fitting it over the
plate and tightening the set screw. When that's secure, add the
rod and the other end unit.* Draw a line around this unit and
proceed as before, but before tightening the screw, insert the rod.

If none of the standard towel rods fit your scheme, buy a longer
one than needed and cut the rod to your liking with a hacksaw.
Installing the john paper holder involves the same procedure,
except don't get too tight a fit or you'll have problems getting the
spring roller in and out.

As you have gathered, I've been talking about additions or replacements of non-built-in fixtures. To replace porcelain fixtures
buried in the wall gets you into tile replacement, too—cold chisel
and all, unless the fixture has fallen out. If it has, you can put in a
new one with cement, as you would loose tile (see page 42). If
the fixture is in tight, unless you have extra matching tile and the
nerves of a diamond cutter, I'd live with it. You can always camouflage it with color-crazy towels, soap or paper.

---

* If you do want to know how good your eye was, you can use a spirit
level and check. If you're really way off, you'd better redo, unless you don't
mind downhill towels.

Windows

ALUMINUM. In many new buildings, the window frames are aluminum. The "pitting" problem is much the same as it is with the furniture (see page 76). A light once-over with a steel-wool soap pad and a couple of coats of good wax, liquid or paste, will make them easier to dust.

CAULKING AROUND FRAMES. Perhaps this sounds nuts to apartment dwellers especially, but if you're tired of the dirt blow marks on the walls around the windows, then caulk. I'm not talking about the outside of the windows and big, old gooey caulking guns. There's a compound that comes in strips in a roll.

Pull off a strip, and with your fingers simply stick along the window frame and wall seam. That's what the directions say. Well, let old sticky-fingers give you a tip. You *know* what it sticks to best. Powder your fingers first. If the area is lengthy, powder periodically and you'll have no problem.

WEATHER STRIPPING. Although basically designed for insulation purposes, this stripping is great as a dirt keeper-outer, too. It's applied either to the window edge itself or to the frame where the window rests when it closes top or bottom. There are all sorts of weather strippings, but the easiest is a plastic polyfoam tape with adhesive backing. Just cut to size and press into place. Do it and toast to another year of clean living, or close to it.

Façades
&
Flourishes

or *How to*

Make the Place

Lovable

The "life can be beautiful" philosophy has come a long way since Great Grandma painted pansies on plates or Grandma* made a darling dressing table out of two orange crates. Besides, they don't make orange crates like that any more; nor pansies, either, for that matter. With so many inexpensive, attractive, colorful, easy-to-use materials and products, you're a dolt if you're living in drear. Operating space is your big problem if you're in an apartment. You seem never to have quite enough room to upheave everything or an out-of-the-way place to do the messier projects. Think positively—with the help of the Sunday edition of the paper, an old shower-curtain liner and a little planning, you can indeed—make the place lovable.

Carpeting

BATHROOM. If hard, bare bathroom floors give you the cold foot, pave a softer way by carpeting. There are enough kinds and colors to confuse Confucius. Personally, I'd vote for indoor/outdoor carpet squares or cotton carpeting. They both do a good job of absorbing water, yet are unaffected by it. I'm not knocking the fuzzy synthetics. I've just always preferred the harder, absorbent squares or cotton. The synthetics can be lovely and soft, but they do not take to water that nicely and feel rather clammy to the wet foot. With carpet squares you can take up the individual pieces that get dirty faster and wash in the basin or easily replace them with others. With carpeting, you can cut a couple of "throw rugs" to fit

* Add a generation, depending on your age.

around the toilet base and toss them into the washer when need be. If you own a dog or cat, a piece of a heavy plastic runner under the newspaper or pan will protect the carpeting.

Find the square footage you'll need by measuring the length and width on the floor. Then multiply the figures. If you have an irregular layout, split the room into regular sections, measure, multiply, then add the sections together to get the total square footage needed.

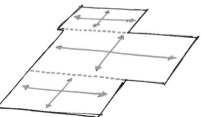

Carpet squares often come in 12″ squares, sometimes 9″. For the squares the dealer has a "converter" that will take your square footage and translate it into the number of squares needed. With squares you'll have practically no waste, although I'd buy extras for color match in case disaster strikes. With cotton carpeting, use the cutouts and leftovers as throw rugs to protect busy areas, for covering scale platforms or as a shock absorber for the top of the toilet tank.

Carpet squares have a carpet-like surface with either a plain or self-adhesive spongy backing. They are very easy to handle because you aren't wrestling with a large bulk of material in a small area. Lay all the full-sized squares you can on the floor following the directional arrows on the backing of each square. The arrows ensure a better texture and color match. If the full-sized squares do not snuggle right up to the wall (blessed be the even-footed room, it's so rare), you'll have to fill in around the edges. Don't trust any wall. It's probably slanty as hell. Sorry, unless your eye is tuned to ¼″ variations (they add up fast as feet run along), you'd better make a paper pattern or measure carefully. You'll be happier.

To fit the remaining areas around such obstacles as the sink, pipes, etc., take the dullest part of the newspaper (not the Sports Section if there's a man in your life) and cut newspaper squares with a carpet square as your pattern. Using the area around the toilet bowl, one of the hardest to cope with, as an example, here's how it goes:

Butt a square of newspaper against the laid carpet squares, crease or draw against the fixture to get the shape you need. Cut out and then double-check the fit. Place the pattern on the carpet and cut with scissors or razor knife. If by some miracle you end up with equal space on each side of the obstacle, just flop the pattern on the carpet square and cut its twin. If not, repeat the process with another square of newspaper. Struggle the rest of the way around in like fashion. If you're stuck with a heavy-footed radiator, exposed pipes or a griffin-clawed bathtub, the idea is to get around it without the necessary cut places showing. Do a little measuring, cut a slit in the square in line with and long enough to go up to the obstacle. Figure the slit to go behind where it won't show much. At the end of the slit, cut a hole big enough to fit around whatever. Start the hole small and try it for a fit. Enlarge it gradually if you have to.

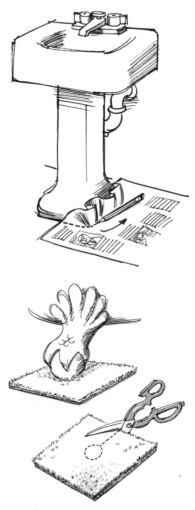

Don't confuse legged wash basins with the above unmovables.

They don't have a fixed idea at all. Meaning, the basins won't fall down when you loosen the legs. The pants are held by set screws (page 12) up tight to the porcelain. They cover the nuts and bolts that hold the legs on. Find the set screw. It should be toward the back but on apartment fixtures it can be anywhere. Loosen, and *voilà!*—down come the pants. Then loosen the nuts a few turns with a wrench or pliers, and the legs will move freely enough to slip the squares under. Straighten the legs, reverse the procedure and you've done it. If you've used squares and any of them shift after they're down, see page 103 for how to anchor them.

Wall-to-wall carpeting. The last two preceding paragraphs about heavy-footed obstacles and legged basins are applicable to all bathroom carpeting. If you buy a prepackaged carpet, which comes in "standard sizes," pattern paper and directions come with it. Measure your bathroom, wall to wall, width and length. Cut the pattern to that size if necessary. Then take the pattern into the bathroom and fit it against the sides where you can. Paste a couple of short pieces of masking tape to hold it to the edges so it won't crawl when you do.

Using the side of your hand, fit the paper up to the front of the toilet. Draw a line along the paper, then pull it back up and cut from the back, straight to the line. Try to aim for the middle. Cut to the right and left along the line. Put the pattern back down, fitting it around the sides. Mark, cut, fit, and so on. If you cut too wide, you can always tape a piece of paper back in to make it right.

When you've finished, lay the pattern on the surface of the carpeting as it would go in the bathroom. Most directions tell you to put the pattern on the back, not the surface of the carpet. This means you have to do mental flip-flops of where the fixtures are. Rather than face that challenge I've found that by securely taping the pattern to the edges of the carpet, I can cut on the surface and prevent the possible confusion. If you order custom carpeting, it doesn't come with a pattern. You can make one by taping sheets of brown wrapping paper together.

Another way is to use the rug itself without the pattern and cut as you go. Essentially you do exactly as you do with the pattern, except that you cut instead of draw. It's chancier but faster, and mostly the fuzz or the nap of the carpet covers any minor lapses.

Usually these carpets stay put pretty well, since the "traffic," although heavy, is not long distance. However, if shifting does occur, you can use double-faced masking tape or sticky carpet tape to stop it.

Note: If you buy one of the cheaper carpetings, allow an extra inch or so for shrinkage when it's washed.

About the scissors. Kitchen utility scissors really do work the easiest, but any good, hefty, sharp scissors will work.

CARPET, KITCHEN. Although many washable indoor/outdoor broadloom types are being widely and avidly advertised, carpet squares really are more practical for a kitchen. Spots around the sink and stove have a way of happening. When the happening is a dropped egg or drooled grease, it's nice to be able to pick up the bad news and scrub it under the faucet. Lots less work, too!

The measuring, buying and installing of the squares are the same as for a bathroom (see page 100), except that in the kitchen you ignore considering the space taken up by the refrigerator. By yourself, you can really do no more than budge it, and who wants carpet under the refrigerator, anyway? Allow for about 3″ under the front so the cheat won't show. A refrigerator is not as flush to the floor as it looks. The squares will slip under the main body and you can chop out little holes to go around the feet. Since the squares won't have an edge to butt up against, they will "walk" unless you're using self-adhesive squares. To prevent this phenomenon here (or elsewhere after you walk on the squares for a while), put down either double-faced masking tape or carpet tape. Use enough tape so that it extends past the edge of the square. Then if you have to pull it up, you can cut through the tape with a razor blade. Work the blade under the tape, then pull it and square up together. Otherwise, when you pull, the tape will stay put along with a great hunk of the rubber backing.

Cords, Disappearing. Are your TV, tape recorder, record player and/or hi-fi components spewing forth wires and cords in Medusa fashion from the wood divider, bookcase, cabinet, wherever? Here are a couple of ways to make them disappear, or at least get them out of the way. First, figure where you want the cords to disappear—out the back, bottom or side. If you have a drill, electric or hand, you can do the whole job with what's called a spade bit. It cuts a nice neat hole up to an inch wide depend-

ing on the diameter of the bit you buy. It's best to begin drilling from the surface that shows most obviously, then if there's any splintering when the bit goes through, it's less likely to show. Or you can use the largest wood bit you have to make starter holes big enough to give your keyhole saw sawing room. The same idea goes even if you don't have a drill.

Pound a large nail into the wood where you want the hole, wobbling it slightly from side to side to keep it loose and to make a larger hole as the starter. If it isn't big enough, pound another hole as close to the first as you can (you may have to crack through any "bridge" with a screwdriver) and saw away. For a really inconspicuous hole, use a bit or nail the diameter of the electrical cord. Cut the cord just above the plug, feed the cord through the hole and rewire the plug (see page 66).

Another neat way to dispense with grangled wires is to wire your end or night tables. Some years ago I bought a table that had this feature and loved it, particularly when trying to cope with a clock radio, a lamp and an electric blanket.

Buy the outlet extension cord (or put one together) designed to mount on the baseboard.

You simply screw it to the underside of the tabletop at the back. Watch the screw length so you don't go through the table surface. This creates a number of outlets on the scene with only one cord going to the wall outlet. If the table is open on the sides, it's easy. If it is closed on the back and sides, figure out where you want to go through and proceed as suggested before.

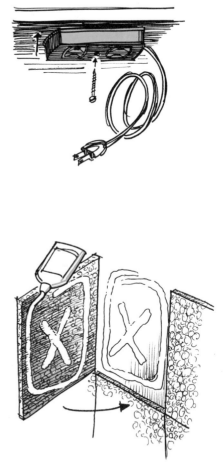

Cork. Dark, chunky Portuguese cork came "in" a few years ago and as a practical prettifier it has more than won its spurs. Ordinary cork also does well and is, in fact, tougher, but most people seem to prefer the color and more varied texture of the Portuguese. You can buy it in sheets or squares; the latter, if you want, with adhesive backing, which naturally costs more. I don't think it's worth it; unadhesive cork is just as easy to put up or on. Use a good household cement or glue, not the lightweight type you most likely have, which tends to be absorbed and is just not hefty enough to hold well or at all, especially on vertical surfaces. You don't have to smear the whole area, just the edges and a crisscross in the middle on both the cork and the surface to be covered.

Do what the glue directions say. Usually it's "let dry until tacky or shiny," and then put the two together. To place it exactly where you want it to go, draw lines if you're not working with edges, because the cork won't come up again. You can do a whole wall, a bulletin board or small table and cabinet tops. It is glorious to use on the top of a bar or server. The cork acts as an absorber and insulator. As mentioned way back somewhere, cork is an attractive way to cover up furniture wounds. One note: New Portuguese cork smells like wet charcoal. The larger the area, the longer the smell hangs on, but it usually disappears after a couple of days.

Curtains, Beaded. Be Sadie Thompson with your kitchen doorway. If you don't remember *Rain* or even Tondelayo in *White Cargo,* you have no idea what a hoot it is to slither through a beaded curtain. I've never yet seen a kitchen door that somehow or other didn't get in the way of traffic or really closed in the smell of liver and onions or boiled cabbage. My solution is to remove the kitchen door and send it into exile. If you're in an apartment, the super will usually bury it somewhere until it's wanted again.

To get the door off its hinges, you have to remove the pins first. Take your hammer and screwdriver. Nudge the screwdriver blade under the lip of the pin on the upper hinge. Hammer upward until the pin moves only part way up. Repeat on the bottom hinge but keep going until the pin lifts out completely. Go back to the top hinge and finish off. This procedure keeps the door from possibly falling on your head.

Lift the door off and be rid of it.

Isn't that a breeze?

Well, not quite. Hinges are the big inheritors of sloppy paint jobs. If you're faced with being unable to find a lip to pound, dig out the paint remover and a cheap water-color brush. Paint the sore spots with remover to loosen the paint enough to get the pin out. Sometimes the paint is so thick that you can chip it off rather than resort to paint remover.

If the leftover hinge parts on the door frame bug you, remove them, plug up the holes with any of the fillers you have on hand, and paint. Actually, when you hang the curtains, these hinge parts don't show that much and only an enemy will notice or say so.

Now, to the beaded curtain itself. If you're a frustrated Campfire Girl or worried about your mental state, you could string one yourself, but it's preferable and eons faster to buy one. And what a choice!—all colors, plus clear, plastic (crystal and opaque) or wood. The shapes, as they hang, range from this to this:

Assembled or strung as you buy them, they are the costume jewelry of your home. Good fun!

The two kinds I've had are (1) a curtain, available in varying lengths and widths, that has a tape with rings on the top to hang from a round rod; and (2) individual strands, available by the yard, to be cut with scissors to the desired length. The latter slide into a slotted rod bought at the same time. The density is determined by how many strands you wish to hang. I did this last one for my bathroom window.

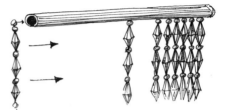

I bought two styles of the crystal version, faceted and round, and alternated them. I put up the slotted rod, then took two lengths side by side, ran them in the slot, cut off at the sill and repeated until I had filled the rod. To figure out what you need for either type, measure the opening and go on from there. Allow extra inches if you want the curtain to go above or wider than the opening. With the individual strands, the manufacturer gives a measurement conversion table for various densities. I found I didn't agree with his idea of dense, so I went back to the well for more.

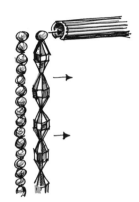

Curtains, No-sew. This may be known far and wide. If so, sorry, but it's well worth knowing to bobbin bogglers like me. Felt is the key. With its no-raveling, wide, wide width and color range, you can cut yourself some curtains.

 Naturally, felt will work for all lengths of curtains. It is relatively heavy, in looks not weight, and opaque. For these reasons (and remember, you don't want to sew widths together), with larger windows it works better as an accent drape on the end with lightweight curtains in the middle.

 For café curtains, cut the felt to the width and length you want. Don't forget to allow enough extra width so that they aren't flat out when pulled together. You want them to hang with some fullness.

 Make a pattern by folding an equal width of newspaper to determine how many scallops you want or how many will work on your window. Remember, you have to start the end with the high area of the scallop and that whatever comes on the fold should be half the width of the ones on the flat. Then when you open the pattern up, the middle will be equal to the others, not twice the size.

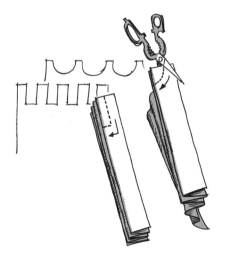

If you're a measuring genius, measure. I've found that good old trial and error combined with just a bit of measuring works better. So much of the look of the scallops depends on the length and width of the curtain, it's hard to judge. That's the reason for the pattern, paper's cheaper than felt. When you're happy with your pattern, fold the felt, put the pattern on top and cut. If you're still not sure of how deep the scallops should be, cut shallow. You can always backtrack and cut them deeper. Cut the other curtains in like fashion. Buy some brass rings of the type that bite into the

fabric ⟨⟩ , not the kind you have to sew on. You can,

but why should you?

The other version of this curtain requires no rings or hooks, and is also shown above. Make this pattern out of newspaper, allowing extra length to compensate for the fold-over required by the loops. The loops' length depends on the air space you want between the rod and the curtains, plus the diameter of the rod. Fold to make the loops, pin to check the looks, cut more if you want to, then glue or use iron-on tape to make the loops permanent.

Floors, Kitchen. The hard-surface floor tile is for those of you who can't *stand* the kitchen floor you inherited and don't want carpeting or carpet squares. Take your measurements as suggested on page 100 and find a flooring store. At almost any given time, they'll be having a "Kitchen Tile Sale." These compare with carpet remnant sales—odd lots, leftovers and nonsellers. If you can't find anything you like, move on to another store or wait it out, new batches come up often. Many kitchens are so small, however, that you can even pay full price and still be ahead.

Choose a tile you can cut with scissors. Buy tile cement and a spreader. Without cementing, lay down as much tile as you can in the wide-open areas, the same as you would for carpet squares (page 100). This will help you figure out where and how much you need to cut the borders and fittings, if any. Don't forget the 3″ or so to slide under the refrigerator (page 103). If the previous floor is tile rather than linoleum, try not to match tile on tile. The stress caused by the pull (quite strong) of the cement will be put in different places. For instance, if "they" started at the sink and ended up with partial tiles at the door, you start at the door and end up with the partials at the sink. This gives you a minimum of seams in common and no corners.

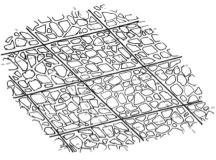

When you're ready to cement, work about two rows at a time by flipping back the noncemented tile and spreading cement on the floor beneath. Spread the cement thin—really thin—or it will ooze nastily around the edges. Press the tile in place. Use a rolling pin or a big soda bottle to make sure the tile is down as tightly as possible. I've done this once in an apartment and heard no squawks from the landlord when I moved. Whether "they" recognized the improvement or just didn't know the difference I wouldn't know. But I can't promise you the same luck.

Fluorescent Lights. I have a blinding hatred of overhead lights, and so, for me, shaded fluorescent lights installed under wall cabinets are a godsend. A like-minded friend touted me on to this solution. Instead of the bare tube light, there is a fluorescent light, approximately 1" deep and in a couple of different overall sizes. Electrical supply and light stores are your best bet to find these. Supermarket-type hardware stores also carry them.

The light has a translucent plastic panel on the front that diffuses the light, with a metal section in the back that has an outlet for appliances. It comes with cord and plug ready to install. If the cord comes out of the side farthest from the closest outlet, the good directions tell you how to change it. I shortened the cord, put on a flat plug (see page 66) and stapled the cord along the underside of the cabinet, but remember to unplug before stapling.

If metal cabinets are your cross to bear, you can drill holes through the metal (see page 3) and use small nuts and bolts to attach the light. Two things here: I'd put a thin rubber sheet (like nonskid pads for throw rugs) or even a shirt cardboard between the light and the cabinet for insulation. Metal on metal and electricity could cause shocks, you know. The other point is, of course, that the nut has to be on the inside on the setting surface of the cabinet. You can work around it, but you may not want to.

Furniture

Refinishing. If you're a perfectionist, my school of refinishing probably is not your bag of tea. I'm all for the shortest, fastest way to wring out the old and bring in the new. I never bother with the parts that won't show. Skip anything you can safely skip, but watch it if you're tall and have a penchant for short friends or vice versa. Church bazaars, rummage and garage sales, Salvation Army outlets, unclaimed freight, second-hand and junky antique stores are natural and fairly cheap hunting grounds for all kinds of furnishings. Almost all furniture pre–1920's, except the posh veneer antiques, is solid wood and a good deal of it oak. Even if you don't like oak's natural light color, you can stain it to various degrees of darknesses. Under a surprising amount of Victorian furniture lurks walnut along with other nice woods. It's just that they had this thing about mahogany stain. Gloom and doom, you know.

To determine whether the piece you've found is veneer or solid wood, scrape a small, unobtrusive spot—on an under edge of a drawer, for instance. A razor blade at right angles or a knife will do the trick. Try to have the courage to do this before you buy. If not, ask. You may get a truthful answer, particularly if you imply that a host of similarly minded friends are awaiting the outcome of your venture. Sometimes the seller will do the scraping for you to prove the piece is what he says it is. If you see , that's veneer, which isn't necessarily bad. It's just fragile. The original purpose of veneer was to achieve beautiful, flawless, matching patterns of wood grains, impossible when wood was taken as it comes. In the twenties, Grand Rapids did furniture no favors when they started using veneer to cover cheap soft woods, which are weak and warp excessively. If you end up with a veneer piece and want to refinish it, the manufacturers of the good finish removers say their products can be used on veneer without loosening it. I'm a coward and have stayed with the solids for a couple of reasons. I like them better and suspect my techniques may be a touch primitive for a layer of wood not much more than 1/16th" thick.

REMOVING THE FINISH. With paint and varnish removers, you indeed get what you pay for. In my experience, the removers that cost a good deal more than the cheapest are worth every cliché penny (to name only one, 5½ gallons of various brands to bring back painted pecky cypress walls horrors!). The better removers have the consistency of a thick smooth sauce. The others are quite watery, which makes them hard to control and especially bad news for working inside around surfaces you don't want affected. Incidentally, turpentine qualifies only as a remover of fresh oil or alkyd paint from you and brushes, not dried painted surfaces.

Buy a cheap flat brush about 3" or 4" wide. Remove any hardware, knobs, or that sort of thing from the furniture to make as many flat surfaces as possible. Open the can of remover. Usually these cans, as do many that contain volatile liquids, have a metal inner liner under the cap in the neck of the spout. To get it out, puncture with the ice pick or a small nail and ease it up and out. The directions warn you to keep your head back. This is good advice. Although the remover doesn't go off like Vesuvius, there is usually a bit of a whoosh with accompanying fumes. Pour a small amount into a flat, wide coffee can you can throw out, or a soup bowl. Removers do not affect metal or china and you can wash it out after. These containers make the solution easy to get to and are the right depth so that you don't overload the brush. Disposable gloves are a good thought, or you may find yourself heading for running water fairly often. Remember, this is a caustic volatile mixture, so take care and don't smoke (see page 31)! Slather on the remover. Too dainty a dose will only tickle the surface. Don't paint the whole thing. Do only as much as you can keep up with. Allow it to set for about ten minutes. Some say less, some say more, but so much depends on humidity, temperature, types of finish and how many layers that it's hard to say exactly. Multi-layers usually need more applications, despite promises, after you've peeled off some of the outer ones.

One thing about paint remover—you certainly can see it work. When the finish is all urky, bubbly and crinkly, scrape a bit off. If the finish really peels off, go! If not, wait a bit and try again. Now, here's where I part ways with most manufacturers of "washable" removers. They say you can use steel wool and water or a scraper (see page 11) to remove the finish. The only luck I've had with the steel-wool and water route is on hard wood like oak in small pieces you can put in the bathtub. Maybe it's me, but I've tried it several times and it's very messy, and on softer woods seems to smear more of the old finish than it removes. I've had good results with a scraper. Scrape firmly and evenly; often using your other hand to "weight" down the blade helps to get off stubborn patches. Don't worry if a little wood comes with it as long as you don't dig at or gouge the wood. Scrape with the grain when you can but it isn't the end of the world if you have to go cross-grain to get at corners and edges. On convoluted parts, you may have to resort to steel wool or a wire brush. Stiff toothbrushes work well, as do grapefruit spoons, knives, screwdrivers. Look at the shape of the problem and try to find something that approximates the shape of what you're trying to clean. If you use any kind of a brush, glasses are imperative. In fact, it's not a bad idea to wear glasses, brush or not. Spatters of this stuff can be mighty mean and downright dangerous to the eyes.

As you work, if the remover dries before you get to it, nothing awful happens. It's just that you have wasted time and remover and will have to start that area over again. If pieces of hardware like knobs and handles need refinishing, pour some remover into a glass just wide enough to accept the piece and deep enough to cover it. For knobs, put the screw or bolt that originally held it in place, back in enough to use it as a finger hold. Pretend you're dyeing Easter eggs. Dip and turn until it's well coated, then put it out on a sheet of foil to "work."

For flat pieces, use a throw-away pie, cake or roasting pan. Scatter the pieces on the bottom and pour on enough remover to cover. Leave these immersed, stirring them around a couple of times, until they are ready to strip. Fish them out and scrape or scrub off the finish.

When you have all the finish off everything or think you do, check for shiny or dark spots. These are spots where the varnish was thicker or less affected by the remover. Scrape until the spot matches the surrounding wood. Apply more remover if necessary.

Take sandpaper, either medium grade followed by fine, or just fine, depending on how roughed-up the surface is. Don't go too coarse or you'll scratch channels in the wood that will be hard to smooth out. If you have big flat areas or enough flat ones where the wood is still spotty, consider renting a hand sander. It's very fast, easy to use and not expensive. After you get over the vibrations, you'll love it for the time and effort it saves. You use the same grades of sandpaper as you would by hand. After sanding of any variety, dust off first with a cloth, then vacuum. The reason for the cloth is that it will catch on any splinters and rough spots to show you where they are. The vacuum picks up all the very fine dust. You want a clean and very smooth surface. Now you should be ready to stain and/or wax or oil. The wood and the color you're after determines which you use.

ANTIQUING. I've done antiquing without the "kits" and I have to admit the results were interesting—not really successful, you understand, but interesting. One chest of drawers ended up looking more solid battleship-gray than "interesting light overtones on a basic dark undercoat." Grudgingly, I recommend the kits. Yea, verily. The kit is more expensive, but all the necessities are there along with pretty good instructions. Without too much experimenting, you, indeed, can "antique" furniture, picture frames or anything your little heart desires.

OIL STAINING. Fortunately, all good oil-stain manufacturers have reasonably accurate color charts, even showing variations on different woods—for instance, walnut stain on oak, pine and birch. An oil stain basically strives to change the color of wood to make it look like another kind. For my money, get pure oil stain without a filler. If you have a nice wood grain, I think filler tends to dull it. Never get stain varnish, or you'll be right back to the grisly, too-bright finish you just worked so hard to get rid of.

The directions with oil stain are clear and accurate. Again resort to gloves unless you like chestnut or walnut or mahogany nails. After the appropriate waiting time, wax and polish, and your masterpiece is done. If the finish has gone darker than you like, ignore the waiting-time recommendations and wax after a few hours. The wax will "pick up" some of the stain and lighten it slightly. Be sure, however, to apply it smoothly and consistently. If the finish hasn't gone dark enough despite repeated staining, use dark wax to begin with and every time thereafter. Gradually the finish will darken.

OILING. If you want a wood finish *au naturel,* then oil (not machine or olive) of some sort is what you should use. There's some goofy mystique about boiled linseed oil. Well, you can have it. It darkens wood considerably, which is fine if that's what you want. But it's sticky to begin with (even cut with turpentine) and gets worse. I think mineral oil is far better. Warm it slightly and rub into the wood with a flannel or soft cloth. For big areas, like those pecky cypress walls I referred to earlier, use an old, clean oven mitt or big canvas work gloves.

Let the mineral oil soak in for a few hours, then wipe down to remove any excess. Wax later if you wish. This is a good idea if the surface is fairly porous or of a softer wood. During the wall project, the drugstore thought I had a terrible digestive problem. After all, how many people buy a half gallon of mineral oil one day and come back for another half gallon the next?

On bare wood, just plain wax is OK, I guess, but it does seem that the stain or oil give the wood finish a subtle depth.

OLD VARNISH FINISHES, PAINTING OVER. Convert, for instance, a mahogany-varnished monster to a talked-about subject. Take steel wool (fine) and dip it in regular vinegar. The cheaper the vinegar, the better; tarragon is not required here. Scrub the piece vigorously. Allow it to dry, then wet-wipe off the residue. Allow to dry thoroughly. This procedure cuts the finish so that the paint can grab hold.

I did this with some dreadful Duncan Phyfe reproduction chairs discarded by a church. To compound the mahogany-varnish sin, the chairs had nasty plum-colored upholstered seats. I scrubbed them down with vinegar, then spray-painted them a wild, clear blue and covered the seats in kelly green. Neither Duncan nor God would recognize them, but the metamorphosed chairs were an eye-popping addition to a country home. Incidentally, the vinegar-and-steel-wool routine is how I prepare for painting over furniture with an old glossy paint finish, too.

Alas, the use of a pad or roller and often the water-soluble paint (pages 127, 131) is denied you, although the semigloss variety is good. The spray (with all its precautions) or the brush is the way to go. Whether you're painting over an old finish or starting with raw wood, here are some suggestions to follow.

Remove all hardware, knobs, hinges and handles, if possible. Again, you may think you can paint neatly around them, but 'taint so. The more uninterrupted flat surfaces you have, the easier and smoother the job.

Fill in exposed, undesired holes. Glue down any split-offs or splinters and sand them smooth. After sanding, dust with a soft, clean cloth and then vacuum to remove all the nitty-gritties.

Take out any drawers and paint them separately. And the same for doors, take 'em off. On better furniture, sliding doors have enough leeway to let you push them up in the top track and get enough clearance to pull them outward at the bottom to remove them. If you can't do this, you'll have to keep shuttling them back and forth until you hit all the spots.

It bears repeating: Don't overpaint!, especially surfaces that move against one another, like drawers, doors and sliding tracks.

Unfinished Furniture

OILING, STAINING, ETC. There are basically two kinds of unfinished furniture. The first, usually of pine or birch, can be painted or stained and waxed. The second, considerably more expensive, is

almost always walnut or teak. Oil with or without wax is all that's
needed to bring out its virtues.

The really cheap unfinished furniture is rarely worth the money.
The pine is of the worst quality, green, liable to severe warping,
and knots which exude a sticky pitch. The workmanship just isn't
there. The doors droop, drawers stick, the whole piece is tacky.
Why spend hours doing a decent job on an indecent piece of furniture? Count your time as money and spend a few more dollars in
the first place.

Pine is softer than birch and as such the stain will penetrate
deeper and darker. However, birch, being the harder wood, holds
up better in the long run.

Sand and stain as described on page 115. You'll find some differences, though. Raw wood tends to be "hairy," has rougher edges
and is thirstier than older, previously finished wood. For walnut or
teak furniture, oiling is child's play, but it should be. You've paid
enough to begin with. You're not trying to change its personality,
you're just trying to bring it out. The materials and procedures are
as before, except that here again you'll find the virgin wood thirstier. It may take a couple of applications of oil so look for dry spots.

There are unassembled, unfinished items of furniture that come
in kits complete with screws, nails, glue and hardware. Most of
the pieces I've seen have more distinction than the less expensive,
unfinished ready-made variety. But stay clear of them if you don't
like jigsaw puzzles. I ordered a Colonial desk by mail (delivered
by truck). With eight drawers, two doors, a pull-out typewriter
platform, supply shelves and a large writing surface, there were
over a hundred wood pieces of all shapes and sizes. All these, plus
about 207 screws, knobs, hinges, brads and sundry hardware,
made for a few interesting evenings. None of these pieces—wood,
metal or nylon—were labeled or numbered specifically, other than
in the directions. The directions were pretty clear, except whoever
wrote them had put this desk together a few times. His semantics,
combined with parts different from those described in the instructions, slowed things down. However, this is the desk I'm
writing this book on. It's holding up better than I am.

PAINTING UNFINISHED FURNITURE. Regardless of the quality
of the wood, smooth well with fine-grain sandpaper. The wood

"hairs" seem to show up more with paint than they do with oil or stain. Probably, the paint makes the "hairs" stand up and be counted. Do use a sealer or undercoat,* either flat white or tinted, the latter particularly if you've chosen darker colors. It's a bore but necessary. It not only gives you a better finished job, but helps you spot any nail holes, bad fits and flaws you missed in preparation. These can be remedied before the finish coat of paint. Before this finish coat, check for "hairs," and sand very, very lightly if any are hanging around.

If the knobs or pulls are wood, make use of their long screws or bolts that attach these smaller pieces to the main piece. For spray paint, loosen them so that the knobs are free to spray behind, around and on.

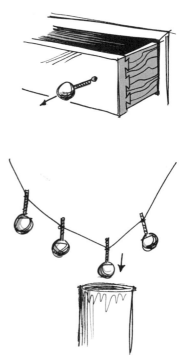

For other paint, remove the pieces and use the screws or bolts as fingerholds for dipping and hanging them to dry. First, string the knobs together about 6" apart with string or wire. Pour paint in a can just big enough for the diameter of the knobs or width of the pulls and deep enough to cover. With a narrow container, you need less paint to get the necessary depth. Dip them one by one, shake or twirl off the excess paint. If you have a large number, limit your "string" to about five in a line to make them easier to handle. Hang

* If you're using spray, it's easier to use the spray for all coats. Actually, you can do this when brushing paint, but usually the undercoat is thinner and cheaper. However, by thinning the "real" paint, you'll have no problem and may even sneak by in some places with one coat.

on a towel rack, shower rod or clothes line to dry. Put a drip-catcher underneath.

In all cases, give the paint more drying time than "they" say, especially in humid weather. You can move the piece into place after it's dry to the touch, even put in the drawers and hang the doors, but don't put felt-based lamps, ashtrays, heavy or sharp-edged objects, newspapers or magazines on the painted surface for at least a couple of days. Although the paint may seem dry, these objects may stick to the surface.

Upholstering. The simple kind, involving tacks and staples, on simple furniture is my speed. As you have gathered, the sewing machine and I were never bosom buddies. When the sewing machine people sing, "It's fun! It's easy! Sew, sew, sew!" So? They are not thinking of me. I once lost a whole size putting French seams in a slip. The point is that for big, all-round, total reupholstering you have to be a sewing nut and a pretty good tailor to battle your way through. You can, however, redo many pieces of furniture by rethinking them. You fold under, tuck and tack where those neat little sewn gussets are, forget cording and that sort of thing. I have done it, but the whole routine is so figure-it-out-as-you-go-along that to try to tell you how would only lead you down the garden path. If you are brave enough to get into it, go to the library and borrow a book on reupholstering. I did. It will take you by the hand through the whole "correct" procedure (parts of which you can ignore). A professional job costs the earth these days. Now, on to the simpler things in life.

CHAIR SEATS, DINING. Upend the chairs, and if the seats do not fall out, you'll be able to see where and how they are fastened. Then, re-move the seat. The fabric or plastic covering is usually tacked or stapled to the board that forms the bottom of the seat. Dig out the tacks or staples with a screwdriver and remove the material to use as

a pattern. Many times it's easier, if the cushioning doesn't have to be replaced, simply to measure and cover right over the old one with the new. If the cushioning has been too thin or is shot, buy either a slab of thick foam and cut to size, or a thin sheet to add to the present cushion. Allow a little extra material when you cut the covering fabric because the new cushioning may be thicker than the old. It will also be easier to grasp the material when you staple or tack it down.

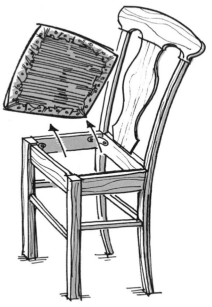

The best way for you to cut foam is to use a razor-blade knife. Draw a line to guide you and cut lightly in short strokes rather than drag the blade along as you would for cardboard. The thicker the foam, the more akin to major surgery it becomes. Use the fingers of your other hand to pull apart the surface of the foam and cut through to the bottom. Don't worry if it isn't exactly straight (it won't be). Foam tends to fill in and compensate for your mistakes unless you end up way off your mark. If you do lose your way, cut off an extra piece of foam and stuff it in the spot as you put the cover on. Use one of the old seats as a guide for folding the corners of the covering material and be sure to pull the material as taut as you

can. Staple and tack down. That's
all there is to it.

BENCHES. These are ideal for
extra sitting space, decoration and
catch-alls, especially in apartments.
You can custom-build a bench by
buying some legs and attachment
plates at some hardware and department stores or lumberyards.
Have the "yard" cut to exact size
1″ (⅞″) plywood. Most will gladly
cut and sell you a custom piece. If
they won't, go elsewhere. A long
bench, 5 feet or over, should have
six legs; for a shorter bench, four
are fine. Screw on the plates that
you can buy with the legs, first in
the corners. Then, if need be, in the
middle of the bench. Screw the legs

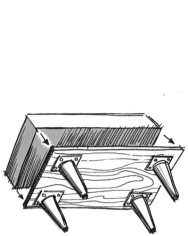

into the plates and set the bench on
its feet. Buy a thick slab of foam.
If you can't find one piece long
enough, buy pieces to make the
needed size and butt them tightly
together. Cut off any extra. You can
also buy the thinner sheets of foam
which come by the yard, and build
a layer cake to the thickness you
want.

Our old friend, felt, is sensational
for benches. Skipping the great
colors and ease of cutting, felt
comes in widths of 96″, which
means you don't have to stew with
seams. Remember this when you
plan your bench. Cut your felt and

proceed as you did on the chair seats, either tacking or stapling the material to the underside. Do one end and a side first so you have something to pull against to make the material taut.

STOOLS. If the stools are already upholstered, follow the same method as you did for the chair seats. If not, and the stools are wood, do a bit of figuring to determine how much material and foam you'll need. Fit, tack or staple on the underside. You'll have to work around the legs, but if you've ever turned a hem, you won't have any trouble.

✿ ✿ ✿

Lining, Drawers and Shelves. Shelf paper that's determined to curl has mercifully given way to color-happy, self-adhesive plastic sheeting. It really is the only thing to use. In addition to being attractive, the surface is smooth enough so that china, metalware and linens can easily be moved on and off it. Since it's nonporous, it cleans with one quick swipe of a damp cloth or sponge.

Linen-closet shelves and just plain shelves are the easiest to do—you've got arm room. If the shelves are removable, remove them. Take their measurements and cut the plastic to fit. The backing of the plastic has inch squares on it to make measuring simple. The last time I used the product, the backing was so crammed with advertising and snappy suggestions for "loads more fun things to do" that I could hardly find the markings, let alone follow them for cutting. It's often easier, faster and less confusing to draw your own cutting guideline.

If the size you're cutting is narrower than the full sheet, try to cut so that you include the starter seam (this is an overlap of the paper backing to help you pull it free) of the paper backing. If you don't have this seam, it's an effort to get the paper backing off. You

can do it by twisting an edge until
the paper tears and you can get a
hold on it and pull it off. Occasionally (I suspect old age and/or
heat) the paper backing does not
come off as breezily as advertised.

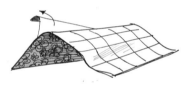

You suddenly have a big island of
paper left right smack in the middle of the sheet. After you stop
swearing, use your fingernail or a
razor blade and very carefully try
to raise enough of an edge to hold
on to. Pull it gently. If you don't
get off all the backing, repeat the
performance until you do.

Anyway, back to the way things
should go. Start at the "starter
seam" and peel off the narrow section. After the plastic sticks to you
and itself (it does that best),
straighten it out and fold this
smaller part, sticky side up, back
over the surface of the still paper-
backed part. Place this on the shelf

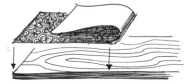

surface so it lines up evenly with
the front edge. Hold that edge
firmly with one hand while you
use the other to smooth the sticky
side in place. Start under the fold
and work away from you until the
exposed side is all down. Be sure
that part is anchored securely, then
lift up the front "flap," turn it back
over the stuck-down portion and
remove the backing. Pick it up by
the back two corners and kind of

roll it out toward you. Smooth it
in place as you go. You shouldn't
get too many wrinkles or bubbles
this way. If you do, pull it back up
to hopefully get rid of the bigger
ones. This material stretches when
you do this, by the way. For small
bubbles, puncture with a pin and
press down.

For drawers, generally follow the same procedure, only on a
smaller scale. The pieces you use may be the remnants from a
larger job, so that you have no starter seam. Do the twist-and-
tear routine. Pull the backing about halfway down and cut off
the majority of it to get it out of the way. Hold the sticky part
up in the air while you position the paper-backed part. Keep
that in place as you smooth the sticky part down, then finish
up as you did for shelves.

Note: This plastic sheeting shrinks about a ¼″ all around after
it's down a day or so. If you have seams or want the plastic
right up to an edge, allow for the shrinkage.

Metal Cabinets, Refinishing. The only really good way to repaint
a metal cabinet is to spray-paint (see page 133), which is almost
impossible on the spot in most kitchens. Epoxy with a brush and
its nail-polish-like flowing qualities is a close second. However,
brush marks will show on the big, flat areas. A bright solution
is to "paper" the door surfaces, either sliding or hinge types. Use
any of the wall coverings described on page 165. The self-
adhesive plastic sheeting will stick like crazy. The others may
give you a problem, particularly around the edges. Rubber
cement will stick down any loose spots. If you use wallpaper
(with its less scrubbable qualities) spray the paper with clear
lacquer before you put it on.

Mirrors, Unframed. If you want to face yourself in the morning,
full-length or eyeball to eyeball, get a mirror. There are some
lovely framed mirrors which, of course, you hang just as you
would a picture. You can hang the unframed ones with the help

of clear plastic or metal holders which often come with the
mirror or which you can buy at the hardware or mirror store.
The number and spacing of these holders depend on the size
of the mirror. For a wall installation, to be on the safe side I'd
use lead shields (see page 16) rather than the lighter plastic
anchors. Mirrors are heavy! On solid wood there's no problem,
just screw in the screws. On hollow doors, be careful. The screws
might hold, and then again they might not.

Decide where you want the mirror, measure and draw a line
where the bottom of the mirror should go.
Install the two holders for the bottom of the mirror so they are tight
enough to set the mirror on. Rest
the mirror on these holders and
draw a line along the top and
sides. Set the mirror aside. Loosely
install the other holders by simply
screwing them in. Measure for
equal spacing. The part of the
holder that the mirror rests on,
not the screws, should line up with
the drawn line. Allow the teeniest
leeway so that the holders don't
"squeeze" the mirror. Glass doesn't
take stress and strain too well. Fit
the mirror into position and gradually tighten each holder in turn.

Paint and Painting

There are several different kinds of paint which we'll dabble in, but there's only one hard-and-fast rule: Don't buy cheap paint. I'll even go so far as to say buy a brand name you know, to protect yourself. If that's on sale, OK, but beware of "unknowns" on sale or otherwise. I don't know what some of the manufacturers put in or don't put in their paint, but what a difference! Good paint goes on easier, looks better, wears better, cleans better, everything better. Cheap paint comes in less than inspired colors, doesn't cover well, is hard to work with and doesn't hold up. If you try to clean it with anything stronger than baby soap, the paint will come off right along with the dirt.

At the paint store or hardware store (watch out for "unknowns" here), you'll find two basic types of paint. There's a third, epoxy, which is quite specialized and as such will be dealt with later. The two are water-soluble (latex and acrylic) and solvent-soluble (oil and alkyd). Although it may be unfair, alkyd isn't my choice. I don't think it flows quite as well or covers as easily as oil paint, yet you still have to use turpentine or a special solvent with it as a thinner and for cleaning up. For doing it yourself, particularly in apartments (where flammables are hard to dispose of), I just don't see using anything *but* water-soluble paints whenever practical. The advantages are numerous.

1. Little, if any, smell
2. Dries fast
3. No lap or brush marks
4. Spatters can be wiped up with damp cloth
5. Brushes or rollers clean up with soap and water
6. *You* can be cleaned up with soap and water

One possible drawback—on older multipainted walls, if one of the coats way down under was early Kemtone or a calcimine paint (a cousin to whitewash), the water-soluble paint may peel and raise. In an apartment, at least you can check with the neighbors to see if they've had any problems. If you're wary, any place, there are two possibilities. Test-paint a small wall and wait for a couple of days and see what happens. The other is to paint with oil or alkyd, using a sealer coat underneath.

Originally water-soluble paints came only in flat finishes, but semi-glossy versions are now available. Although I'm not overly fond of shiny finishes, they really are better for kitchens, bathrooms, doors, windows and woodwork. Grease, champagne spatters, make-up, soot and greasy little fingerprints wash off better. But here again, if you, too, have a thing about gloss, go ahead and use the flat variety, figuring you can always slap another coat of paint on without making a big production out of it.

Epoxy is a paint you may or may not want to have an affair with. It's a little finicky but marvelously tough. Epoxy is so shiny it looks like lacquer. It depends on a chemical reaction for its virtues, so you have to mix it at the time of use and only the amount you will use. I've painted a bar with epoxy, as well as bathroom tile (see page 141). If you think of epoxy as going on like nail polish, you're half way to handling it and to doing a good job.

When you buy your paint, have the store put it on their shimmy machine; although most will offer to, you may have to prod some. This mechanical stirring mixes paint well and saves you the mess and the time. If you don't have this done or have put off the painting, stand the can on its head the day before. This starts the heavy sediment moving. Some paints are homogenized, or close to it, and have the consistency of loose mayonnaise. Even after some months I haven't noticed that these settle, but a stir to make sure never hurts.

The paint store almost always throws in a stir paddle for free. If they haven't, use something nonporous like a glass stir rod or a slotted cooking spoon. You can wipe or wash it clean.

Applicators. Of the five possibilities—bristle brush, polyfoam brush, pad, roller and spray—which is the best way to get your job done? Much of the choice depends on what you're going to paint. Generally the slowest is the regular brush or the polyfoam version, the simplest the pad, the fastest the roller, the trickiest the spray. Let's compare.

BRISTLE BRUSHES. As might be expected, good quality will make for a better end result. But you don't have to get carried away. Just don't go so cheap that you spend more time fishing bristles out of and off of, than you do painting. If what you're doing (such as shellacking gooey knotholes before painting) almost decrees throwing the brush away after you've finished, don't splurge. With water-soluble paint, however, the brush will clean up so well that getting a good brush is worth it. You won't even be tempted to do a mediocre cleaning job or to leave the brush until tomorrow.

It pretty much follows that "natural" brushes (made from various unlucky animals) work best with "natural" oil-based paints. The synthetic brush co-ordinates well with water-soluble. Honest-to-goodness painters tell me paint remover eats these synthetics alive. I don't know, but those 5½ gallons of remover I mentioned all went on with one cheap synthetic brush and it's still bristling. Regardless of natural or synthetic bristles, brushes are designed for specific painting assignments, but don't be burdened with guilt if you use one for other than the stated purpose.

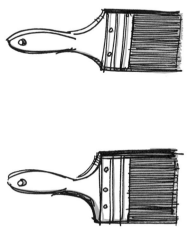

The wide, thin, flat brush, works well with paint remover and thinner liquids like oil stains, shellac and protective clear plastic coverings over other finishes. This brush doesn't take on too much of a load, which reduces dripping with the thinner liquids and gives you a broad, fast coverage.

Wide thick brushes are for larger surfaces and areas. The width usually ranges in graduated sizes from about 2½″ up to 5″. These brushes hold a fair amount of paint and put it not too delicately where you aim. With discretion and practice, you won't get too many drips and can make this brush paint

up to many an edge without slop-
ping over where you don't want it to.

The narrower, fat brush is for
moldings, window and door details,
narrow spots and places where you
want control and accuracy.

You'll do a neat and smooth job all the way if you keep a couple
of thoughts rolling around in your head. Don't drown the brush
in paint. Dip it about one-third of the length of the bristles. Get
rid of the excess by slapping, or dragging, against the inside of
the paint container, whichever comes naturally. Real painters
say don't drag the brush. They're probably right, but guess which
you'll do. By not overloading you avoid splats on the floor and on
you, runs down the handle of the brush, paint sags on the
surface and drips on edges

. Use light, smooth strokes, and let
the paint flow on. Don't try to scrub it in. You're trying to put
paint *on*, not in!

POLYFOAM BRUSHES. When is a
paint brush not a brush? When it's
one of the relatively new polyure-
thane foam brushes. They're available in varying widths and designed
to be used and thrown away. Some
come with permanent handles and
a brush/pad that snaps on and
off. With others, you throw the
whole thing out when you're
finished. An article extolling the
virtues as well as the differences
of this "brush" led me to try it. I
can't say I was all that taken with
it. True, you don't get brush marks,

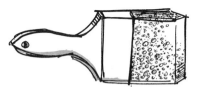

because there aren't any bristles. But for obvious reasons, it acts as a single unit without the flexibility of the individual bristles, which help you paint in corners and smoothly along edges. But give the polyfoam brush a try, especially if you haven't painted much with a brush and have no preconceived notions about how it should act, and it's cheap.

PADS. It beats a four letter word out of me, Lieutenant, what to tell you to ask for if you want one of these. Paint pad or coater might do, but sign language, drawing a rudimentary picture or simply pawing through the store are the only ways I've found so far. There is a bunch of grabbing brand names like spelling coater with a K, but I seem never to find the same one twice. Persist—for many jobs it's worth the confusion. As far as I know, this gimmick was originally designed to paint shingles, but I've used it on smoother inside surfaces like ceilings and walls. The pad is a kind of cross between a brush and a roller. You can use it with a roller pan (see page 136) or a special "bucket" you buy at the same time you buy the pad. The texture and consistency of the actual pad is like a soft crew cut with a thick foam backing that gives it enough resil-

ience to press in and cover uneven surfaces. The pad is flat, about 3″ by 5″, and either slides onto the handle part from the end or snaps onto the sides. You more or less "pull" paint on. You'll get what I mean when you use it, but it's a heal and toe action with the spring in the handle moving things along. This gismo is *not as fast* or quite as smooth as a roller, but it doesn't tend to splatter as much. It also has beveled edges that can move right up to corners without the brush fill-in required by a roller. The pad covers *faster* than a brush but takes more huff and puff because it's a pulling-and-pushing action rather than a gliding or flowing one. The pad washes easily and well when used with water-soluble paint. With the other kinds of paint, forget washing the pad and toss it out.

ROLLERS. You can buy rollers in various lengths and surfaces. The surfaces range from hard and short like mohair to a soft, fleecy deep lamb's wool. The shorter-haired types are for glossy paints and/or a smoother finish on the wall. The woolies are good for a touch of texture on smooth walls or "filling in" pock-marked, uneven or porous walls. Unlike a brush, it can be "rolled" in all directions, up, down, back and forth, diagonally, which-

ever or all to give you the best coverage. There are two drawbacks to
a roller. The first is that it tends to
spatter teensie, teensie freckles of
paint around. The faster you roll,
the more so. Subdue the urge to
spin off the end of a stroke with
a flourish—this just adds more
freckles to the surroundings. The
other is the roller's inability to get
next to a corner, a ceiling line or in
small areas. It's the design, of
course, but there's no way around
it, a roller won't roll otherwise. This
means you have to fill in with a
brush and use a corner roller,
shaped like a small, fat wheel.

With water-soluble paint, you
can do all the edges and corners
first with a brush and the corner
roller, then take to the wide roller
for the big areas. With oil paint,
you have to do these parts as you
come to them or the lap marks and
texture differences will show.

SPRAY. Spray paint is unruly for
two reasons: its drift and speed.
The *drift* can be a problem unless
you have, or can make, a windless
area or one where it doesn't matter
where the paint lands. The carrying
distance of this paint seems farther
than the Wright brothers' first flight.
Spread newspapers or a paint cloth
at least 5 feet in all directions. Open
any windows that don't directly

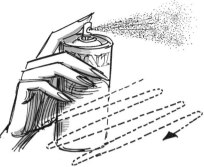

affect the spray. Don't smoke. Get out of the area often for fresh air if the job goes on, and open any of the closed windows between sprays. Better yet, wear a man-sized handkerchief as a "mask" to keep from inhaling the very fine spray. Naturally, if you can go outdoors (pick a windless day) or to a basement, do so.

The *speed* of the paint coming out can be a problem until you get used to it. You have to keep moving, or too much paint will land too fast in one spot and will cause sags and drips (page 130). The directions on the can are clear and should be followed. Nevertheless, the first burst out of the can will be a bit unnerving. Start on an unshowing place or a piece of cardboard to get the knack. It's really not hard. Spray paint is absolutely the greatest for chair rungs, legs, wicker, bamboo, convoluted and louvered anything. It's expensive in proportion to the quantity of paint. But handled properly, less covers more and hard-to-paint-by-hand items are slick and easy with spray paint.

SOME MEANINGFUL EXTRAS

A *paint-drop cloth* isn't cloth for us amateurs. It's a large, usually 9′ x 15′, sheet of lightweight plastic or heavyweight, tear-resistant paper. Or if you're as smart as a friend of mine, you save your old shower-curtain liner and use it instead of buying a paint cloth. Putting down the store-bought "cloth" is somewhat like putting down the tarp on a rainy night at the local baseball stadium. Only, it's easier for the crew there because they don't have protruding objects

like lamps, tables and chairs. But for big jobs, particularly drippy ceilings, a paint cloth is worth it. For small jobs, newspapers are just dandy. I discovered a fringe benefit of the plastic paint cloth last summer. Five guests had way overstayed their visit because of a continuing heavy rainstorm. When they simply had to leave (yawn, yawn) they used the paint cloth as an all-encompassing umbrella. The effect was a bit like a Chinese New Year dragon, but it kept all but feet dry.

Paper buckets come in two or three sizes, are inexpensive and simply great even for other reasons. You can use and toss with impunity. The top diameter is beautifully wide, so you don't have to aim the brush to keep it from catching on the bucket edge. This catching louses up the bristles and spatters paint. Paper buckets are also excellent for wallpaper paste.

If you have a plastic household bucket, it can be used for water-soluble paint or wallpaper paste. Just be sure it's clean, with no silt grinding around in the bottom. Wash it out after you've finished the paint job, and it goes back to its other life. Big juice cans and coffee cans earn their keep for smaller paint jobs and cleanups.

Roller pans are exactly that— medium, sturdy metal pans designed to hold paint so the roller can get to it. They are slanted to maintain a "well" of paint at one end with a gradual, cleated incline to even out the paint and remove the excess on the roller. These pans can be cleaned and reused. One suggestion most painters make is to line the roller pan with foil, which you can pull up after painting and throw away. Certainly for oil and alkyd it's a big plus, but I don't bother for water-soluble paints.

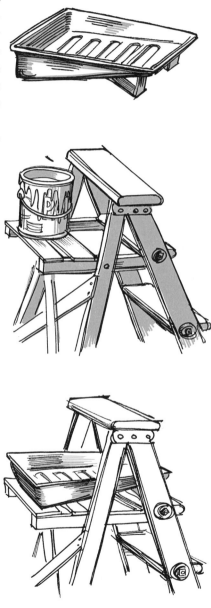

A genuine *stepladder* can be a tremendous lift for painting skyward. Not only in the reaching-on-tiptoe department, but the flap-down part will hold the paint bucket. If you're using a roller tray, place it on the flap and pull it through so that the back legs rest on the step. The up-and-down-the-steps routine is wearing enough without your having to come down for paint. Why is it the whole world calls you on the phone when you're doing your high-altitude act?

An *edge guard* is theoretically designed to keep paint away from places where you don't want it, like windows, floors, etc. I say "theoretically" because I once used one manufactured out of a short piece of Venetian blind with a handle attached. If I didn't remember to wipe it off I smeared more paint around than if I had gone my own slovenly way. A laundry cardboard, tablet backing or folded paper does as well or better, since it absorbs the paint to a degree. You can use all the edges and cut off or fold the wet paint parts for a clean edge. On windows I just don't bother. Persnickety types go for the edger or masking tape. Putting the latter around every little edge is more tedious to me than scraping off the excess later with a razor blade.* With a little care, practice and a narrow brush you really can stay on line surprisingly well.

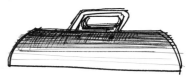

On wood, you can wipe up the paint immediately, or if there are lots of little speckles, you can get those off later with a light rubbing with steel wool. Paint really doesn't want to stick to waxed surfaces.

PREPARATION. The less clothing you wear, the better. Painting is always hot, unless you're doing a cold barn. Sneakers, definitely. A hat or bandanna, a Mother Hubbard–type shift (a wide skirt so your knees don't bind and you fall flat), shorts or jeans and a shirt serve splendidly for uncaught drippings and unthinking hand wipe-offs. If you've been a good girl and gotten all the needed supplies, you may not have to appear in public in your regalia.

---

* Chances are you've had scraping practice if you've ever moved in after a "professional" painter has been at it. In one apartment I never took reading material to the bathroom for over three months, only a razor blade to clean the tile of paint measles while I contemplated. Guests were never required to participate.

Hopefully, before you're standing there with paint on your brush, you've done any hole and crack filling, and sanding thereof. Loose paint should be chipped out or scraped off, then either sanded close to even with the wall or spackled in and sanded. If you face an old paint blister or a curling crack where

the paint has semi-lifted   , hit it with the handle of your putty knife. Knock the paint off, back to where it is solid to the surface, then fill and/or sand. For glossy painted walls that haven't the wear of the ages, it's best to wash them down with a strong mixture of vinegar water. For really greasy or dirty surfaces, a quick wipe-down with a strong mixture of detergent and water is a must.

Before you pour paint from the can into a roller pan, bucket or another can, press foil or stick masking tape in the groove where the lid fits. This keeps paint from getting into the actual groove. When you're finished you can pull up the liner along with its paint pool and replace the lid tightly and neatly. Hammer the lid lightly all around the edge to seal it well. If you haven't done the foil or tape routine, put the lid on gingerly and cover it with a paper towel or cloth. Then tap. If you don't—squirt! As you can see, I've had practice. Half the time I forget to be neat ahead of time.

Painting a Room. I almost always paint the parts first that I hate the most. For some strange reason this coincides with how you're supposed to do it. Imagine! The ceiling, then the walls, doors, windows and baseboards come last. The reason for this order is based on using different paints for the different parts of the room. But if you use the same paint for all, do it any way you want. I suspect you will hate ceilings, too. If you can rationalize that they really don't need painting, do so with alacrity. This goes double for closets, which you handle like little rooms, except that they're more crowded and rarely have windows. You can paint before the real room or after, whichever suits your fancy. I usually do them first, if at all, because the dust raised (gesundheit!) is considerable.

THE CEILING. If there's nothing you can do about it but paint, clear and cover an area with a painter's cloth or newspapers so you can work across the width of the room. Unless you have ape arms, figure to cover 4 to 5 feet before you'll have to move the ladder. Don't brush the paint on unless it's a small ceiling. Use the roller if you can. It's faster, smoother and easier. There are extension handles for rollers, but the extreme length of the handle adds a curious lack of touch that makes the operation rather unwieldy. I did find, though, that by adding one section to the handle of the roller (the extensions come in three sections) and using the stepladder, I kept control, yet minimized the need for dizzying heights and overextended reaching.

If you can, try to stay with the painting long enough to complete the whole ceiling. You'll be tempted to throw in the roller. Experts caution that it will show where you stop and then start again later. Foo! With water-soluble paint and your own uncritical eyes (nobody else will dare criticize), stop if you really poop out. It's better than falling off the ladder. However, take a breather, and if you can, keep on going. You'll be so happy when it's finished you'll be delirious.

When painting the ceiling, paint down onto the wall about an inch or two, even if you're painting the wall a different color. In fact, more so if there is a color switch. This rounding of the bend down onto the wall means you don't have to do an extra-steady hand act trying to keep the paint off the ceiling.

Unless the ceilings are really hopelessly dirty, you can get away with one coat most of the time. If you find thin or show-through spots, don't be ashamed at all to double-coat those and forget the rest. The total effect blends and the ceiling is a long ways away. If the whole ceiling looks like a spotted cow, then do a second coat. But try the shortcut first. It's a lot less wearisome. The same goes for walls, too!

WALLS go much faster. Could be gravity, but something speeds up the action when you're on the vertical. Maybe it's you, glad to use your arm in a more normal manner. Again, try not to stop in the middle of a wall. However, if you get a sudden dinner invitation, go! With walls you have more natural stopping places than on ceilings and you can usually make it to an edge or a corner. *Note:* If you're worried about running short of paint, do indeed follow this scheme. Paint, like yarn, is made in color lots and as such can vary slightly, even though carrying the same label. Even when paint has been custom-mixed you're taking a chance if you change from one can to another in mid-wall. But again, don't fret—if it happens, it happens. By the time you put a sofa, a picture, a lamp or a chair on the scene, who's to know?

ALL THAT OTHER—DOORS, WINDOWS, BASEBOARDS. Most home experts devote pages to the exact step-by-step don't-you-dare-do-it-differently way to paint doors and windows. I don't know, I just paint them. Use a roller or pad on any flat, wide parts. (Despite other dubious advantages, hollow, flush doors are a blessing. You just roll right over them just as if they were a wall.) For the other squiggly places and narrow spots, use a brush before or after the roller. Have patience. Remember to sand, scrape, fill or putty wherever needed before you start painting. These spots are where you'll often find loose, curled surplus paint, caused by water, telephone cords, dried putty, dirt. Another only-too-common problem is flaked-off paint, particularly in newer paint jobs. This is caused by a combination of green lumber (not seasoned) and bum paint.

Watch out for drips and runs in the corners if the door has panels. On windows, comparable danger spots are the cross bar moldings and corners.

With double hung windows, I usually paint the top of the upper sash first, pulling it clear of the main frame. Then pull the top sash on down within a couple of inches of the sill and push the bottom one up out of the way. Paint what you couldn't reach before, then push this sash back up, still clear of the frame. Paint the bottom sash and then the frame and the sill.

Although most "pros" paint every surface they can get a brush on, don't unless you have to. They do the underside and front of the bottom of the top sash; the bottom side of the bottom sash; the "channels" the windows slide up and down in.

If you've ever inherited multicoated windows, you already know the problems. The paint of the ages makes windows stubborn and sometimes impossible to open without major surgery. They get worse with each new coat of paint. If you are dealing with brand-new wood, the area should be protected with a primer and finish coat of paint to keep it from swelling with moisture. But easy does it.

Remove any hardware you can. Painting around it is difficult and you'll probably get paint on it, anyway. If you can't get the hardware off because of those who have gone before you, use paint remover to get to the screws. Or give up, join the group, paint over the hardware and worry about it next year.

FLOORS. One good thing about floors, the paint won't drip on on you. But clearing a large area can be difficult. Usually it's better to do only half the floor at a time. Move the furniture, lamps, etc., to one end while you work at the other. If a rug is involved, fold it back and weight the end down with a piece of furniture. Don't put anything heavy or step on the fold of the carpet, or you could break its backing. Use the same discretion on drying time as you do for furniture. Watch the moving of furniture across the surface, don't drag it, ever. There are special, tough, wear-resistant paints for floors. Choose accordingly for cement, linoleum or wood.

PAINTING CERAMIC TILE. This two-coat epoxy paint job is only worth sweating through if you own your own place. If the tile is a dreadful color and/or old and crazed (that's those fine little cracks and lines under the surface—you've probably seen this phenomenon on old china), then contemplate using epoxy paint. Tearing out old tile yourself is a time-consuming mess, requiring a cold chisel, a hefty hammer, safety glasses and the proverbial patience of Job. Because tile doesn't come off cleanly or evenly, you still have a problem of patching and plastering afterward, even before you begin to retile.

Epoxy paint over tile is not as tricky as it is meticulous. Epoxy creates a very tough, hard, shiny surface and you're applying

it to a similar tough, hard, shiny surface. To get it to stick and
stay stuck is the hard part. First, the old tile has to be clean,
clean, clean. The dirt, soap scum and grease must be removed
(see page 42). Scrub the joints and seams with scouring powder
and a toothbrush. The directions on the paint suggest you "rough
up" the tile surface with sandpaper or other abrasives before
painting. I tried this and didn't make a dent so I stopped, because
it's very hard to be sure the tile is "sand" free after.

Before painting, wash down all the tile with the epoxy thinner.
This is very heady, even headier than the paint itself. Get as
much air moving through the room as possible. Don't smoke!
Get out every ten minutes or so and clear out your lungs.

This is a two-part on-the-spot chore. Mix strictly according to
instructions, because the proportions of paint are important. Mix
the paint and start in. Paint behind the toilet or under the sink
or behind the door first. In other words, any place that's not too
visible or reflects light, until you get the knack of the paint, then
launch out from there.

As I said elsewhere, epoxy is much like nail polish. It dries fast
so watch out for brush marks, and don't brush too thin or back
and forth too often or you'll gum up the works. Try to get the
first coat even, but don't worry too much if there are thin spots
or some brush marks. They'll fill in with the second go-around.

PAINTING A RUG. This sounds wild and it is—but it works. I
know of two ways. One I've done, the other I've seen the results
of. Begin with a rug you've given up on for one reason or another.
It's a little wopsey; the backing has lost its stiffness; it's worn
down to the warp or it still has a lot of wear in it but you hate it.
The two case histories will explain. The first rug was advertised
as an all-wool gold-and-cream twist. I suspect cotton was hiding
in there somewhere because I never saw any carpet get dirtier
faster. It was not worn out, in fact it refused to be. The decision
was to move it to the enclosed porch of a lake house and paint
it black.

I doubt painting would work on anything but a twist, a short
or no-nap. Big loops or cut pile would probably mat and stick
down. You need a "stand up on its own" surface or practically
none at all. I also doubt that paint would take to the synthetic
rugs. Maybe, but I leave that to your noble experiments.

I started by looking for what seems now to be "old-fashioned" rug stain. It was designed way back to rejuvenate fiber or straw-porch rugs. I found people who'd heard of it, yes, it was still being made, but by gosh, don't know, etc. After some cogitating, I decided on a good-quality oil-based paint. I thinned it way way down to a watery consistency, with solvent, creating my own stain as it were. I bought a scrub brush and a throw-away roasting pan and proceeded to scrub the paint in. Use a nonabsorbing glove for this job, or you'll be black (or some color) up to your wrist. The scrubbing action raised and separated the fibers as well as allowed the "stain" to penetrate to the warp. I did about a 2' x 2' area at a time. The rug was thick and the floor below didn't matter, so I didn't bother with any kind of protection underneath. I would advise using a painter's cloth or newspapers underneath if you want to protect the floor.

Drying time is anybody's guess, and the rug should not be walked on at all until it's bone-dry. The thick rug I did with windows open on a sunny dry day was OK for walking on in eight hours. Test the surface with your hand, brushing across and pressing down. No doubt, the longer you can stay off of it the better it will be.

Know this! The surface of the rug is not as soft as it was before, but it is still quite resilient. Two years later, with much tracking in, out and on, the rug is beginning to show its true colors in heavy traffic areas. So? I'll paint it again.

The second example was a huge oriental rug worn nap-bare but still holding tenaciously to its basic pattern and strength. Friends of mine bought a batch of marker pens close to or matching the original colors and had a group in for a color-the-carpet party. Crazy like foxes, they staved off buying a new rug for a couple of years.

CLEAN UP. On layers of newspaper "paint" as much of the paint out of whatever applicator you've used. With water-soluble paint, after you've "painted" it out, simply wash with warm water and soap. With a brush, be sure you get into the middle of the bristles and near the handle. The water should be clear when you squeeze the brush. Wash until it is. Allow it to dry, wrap in foil and store.

With a roller, I usually lean it under the faucet and let the water run down over it for a while. This washes a good deal of the paint away. Then I take the roller off the holder and finish up with soap and warm water. Stand on end to dry so you don't flatten the nap. It's best to set the roller on a paper towel for draining. Cleaning a paint pad is the same as a roller. Here you rest it on its back for drying. Once either of these is thoroughly dry, I've never found it mattered whether it sat on its nap or not.

For oil or alkyd paint, use turpentine, the recommended solvent on the paint can, or one like benzene. If you've used a roller or pad, toss it out. It takes forever to clean it.

If you've used a brush, "paint" most of the paint out of it on a newspaper. Pour a small amount of solvent in a juice or coffee can. Work the brush back and forth in the solution to make sure it gets between the bristles. Paint the newspaper until the brush is dry. Pour clean solvent in another can and repeat. By now the brush should be clean enough to wash with soap and warm water. It'll take a while before the soap will suds, but it will, so keep washing until it does. When all traces of the paint are gone, shake the brush and shape the bristles together and either hang or lay the brush down to dry. Once dry, it's better to wrap the brush in foil to hold its shape.

Use some care disposing of this highly flammable solvent. In an apartment, I've labeled it FLAMMABLE and set the can where the trash is collected or personally given it to the porter. Never, never throw the can down the incinerator. In a house, I've set the can outside in some safe place. The solvent will evaporate rapidly, leaving only the dried sediment, which you can put in with the trash.

If you're stopped in the middle of a painting job, rather than go through the clean-up, wrap the roller or brush in foil or a plastic bag. For a couple of hours this will keep the paint from drying. Some of the paints dry so fast that you'd better wrap them even for a coffee break.

With Oil or Alkyd paint, you can leave brushes in a can with solvent overnight. Be sure to "paint" out the excess solvent on newspaper before starting to paint for real again.

To get yourself cleaned up, either wash with soap and water or use the same solvent you've used with the paint, then wash.

LEFTOVER PAINT. Air acts on paint in a can, just as it does drying on a wall but more slowly. If you have considerable paint left over and a fair amount of "air space" above it, store the paint in Mason jars with rubber seals around the lids. These are the jars your ancestors and some sturdy types today "can" food in. Surprisingly, you'll find these in many hardware stores and houseware sections, and maybe not so surprisingly in gourmet cooking supply stores. Almost as good as these, especially if you put a plastic sheet between the lid and container, are glass food or juice bottles. Try to get a close "fit" for the paint, a jar where the paint comes close to the top. The less air space, the more slowly the paint will thicken and form a skin on the surface. Label what kind of paint it is and where it was used. You'd be amazed how cloudy the memory gets after a few months. A good clue: if commercial painters are doing your job, ask them for some of each color and/or finish. Store as above for patch-ups and match-ups.

If there is too little paint to save and the color is important, smear a dab on white paperboard or even paper. Write brand, type, color and/or number on the back, so if you want that paint again, you can get a close match.

Paneling, Wood. If you're suddenly seized by a mad desire for the rustic warmth of a wood wall, you can be soothed. An amazing assortment of real wood grains are now available in panels or sheets. Measure the width and length of area to be wooded and choose your medicine. You can literally paste many of these to any relatively even wall with a special cement. Another way is to use furring strips (rough lumber strips about 1″ x 2″ thick), which you put up at approximately 18″ intervals with plaster nails. These strips support the paneling. Then you nail, with finishing nails, the paneling to the strips. The lat-

ter is a bit drastic for renters, but again, you can remove and repair the wall to avoid the wrath of the landlord.

Pegboard. Even a foot-wide piece of pegboard (see page 28) placed between the upper cupboards and the counter can be a help in a drawer-poor kitchen. It can carry a spice shelf, bottle opener, measuring cups, measuring spoons, tongs, or larger utensils if you have a lot of space. Many items, of course, come with hanging racks, but your wall will look like a shooting gallery if you use them all. The pegboard makes a unit out of lots of littles.

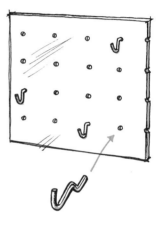

You can buy a pegboard "kit," but for little trouble and less money you can get *exactly* the size you want by going to the lumberyard. They often have a scrap bin where you might find just what you need, or most of them will cut the pegboard to size for you.

Pegboard has to be set out from the wall so that the hooks have a space to lock into. This is accomplished by anchoring the pegboard on small, hollow cylinders called spacers. Most lumberyards have these spacers as well as the various hooks and hardware. If they don't, hardware or houseware stores usually have what you want. Fiber plugs and plastic anchors are strong enough for installing pegboard.

Hold the pegboard up where you want it. Use an ice pick or anything that will mark the holes in the four corners, the middle holes and more if the pegboard's a long one. Drill (page 4) or pound a nail, wobbling it to keep it loose to make holes for the plugs (page 16). Put the plug in, the spacer over it, the pegboard in place and screw through the hole, through the spacer into the plug. Sometimes the spacers are hard or nigh-on to impossible to hold on to, particularly when you're up close to either the cupboard or the counter or in the middle of the pegboard. See trouble coming. Curved tweezers work sometimes if you have three hands. Better yet, don't tap the plug all the way in. Leave just enough hanging out to give the spacer something to catch on while you perform magic with the screws. Paint the board before or after installation, whichever seems easier to you. If you're using spray paint, definitely before. If any of the holes fill up (there are usually some ornery ones), clean them out with a cotton swab, toothpick or kitchen match.

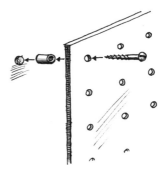

Picture Mounting

HOMEMADE FRAMES. I'm no closer to cutting a good miter than a sinner to a bishop. If you prefer frames with such corners, I suggest you buy one that's ready- or custom-made.

Cutting a miter looks deceptively simple. You think you just saw two pieces of wood at the same angle and put them together. Not so! It involves all sorts of figuring of angles as well as a miter box. I bought a thing called something like "Miracle Miter Master" and I can't even figure it out, let alone use it.

A friend of mine was going to miter some quarter round molding (see page 30) to go along a radiator cover. The job required two 15″ strips and one 54″. He started with two 8′ strips of molding. By the time he finished he had not one usable piece and had sawed partway through the stepstool as well. Mitering is most frustrating and I urge you to forget it.

For canvas on wood stretchers or anything mounted on at least a ⅜″ board of some sort that can be nailed into, you can make a frame out of flat wood strips or 1″ x 2″ lumber. Saw two strips to the measure of the sides of the picture, plus the depth of the wood edge.

For instance, if the picture is 20″ and the edge is ¼″, the length to be sawed would be 20½″. The top and the bottom strips are sawed to the picture size. This puts the seams where they show the least. For the heftier lumber, glue and nail together with small finishing nails (see page 21). For the lighter-weight wood, good epoxy or wood glue should do, unless the picture itself is quite heavy. To get and keep a "square," either draw a form on paper or use the picture as the "mold." It depends on your neatness with glue factor. Mine's low, so I use the paper pattern with wax paper over it at the corners (so I can see through) where I glue. It has less tendency to stick to the frame. When it is dry, paint or stain the frame. Use small finishing nails to fasten the picture in.

READY-MADE FRAMES. When you buy a ready-made frame or a ready-to-put-together frame whether it's wood, metal or Lucite, finish or paint it first if need be. If you want a covering glass and it didn't come with the frame or the store couldn't supply it, go to a glass-and-mirror store.

Have them cut a glass to the dimensions of where the glass and picture will rest in the frame minus ⅛″. This allowance means you won't have to force the glass into the opening. It doesn't bend all that well, you know. Even though prints of oil paintings (like the originals) are not supposed to be glassed over, dirt and humidity being what they are can make this a good idea.

Take the picture and trim off only enough to fit it into the frame opening. Hold off cutting if you're going to use a matte. That's a picture-enhancing border of colored or white board, theoretically never used with oil paintings or prints of same. It ain't necessarily so! Make an exception if a small matte painted gold or black or covered with linen can make it look like part of the frame edge and save you the cost of a new dress worth of custom framing. You can buy matte board at any good art store. Some will even cut the matte to exact size for you.

To cut a matte yourself, first, trim the outer length and width to the inside dimension of the frame. Measure the picture to find the size of the opening you will want to cut in the matte board. You may want to do some juggling to get a wider bottom on the matte. This old-fashioned rule for nonsquare pictures often does something for the picture. However, to accomplish this, the top should not be narrower than the sides, so ponder a bit.

When you decide, measure in from
the outer edges of the matte, lightly
mark and then draw lines, using
a yardstick, where the opening is
to be. Place the matte on a heavy
cardboard for cutting. Take your
razor-blade knife and yardstick or
a suitable straightedge and cut out
the hole. Two cautions: Put the
yardstick on the outside of the line.
First, in case the blade slips, you
cut into the board you're not going
to use. Second, you can see when
you're coming to the corners which
you don't want to cut past. Bear
down heavily on the stick so it
won't move. First time around, cut
lightly with the blade to make a
track for the blade to stay in and
then bear down to cut through.

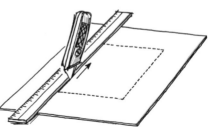

Professional matte cutters bevel these edges; i.e., they slant the
blade to get an edge that slants like so   instead

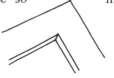

of   To keep the angle of the blade consistent is a
neat trick. Since I waver, I've contented myself with straight
up-and-down edges. So far nobody's even noticed the difference.
If you have any "hairy" edges, sand them slightly with an emery
board. The insides of all this board, regardless of outside
color, are whitish. If you're using a colored matte and mind the
white showing, run a flow pen of a contrasting or matching color
around the raw edge. Trim the heavy cardboard you've been
cutting on so that it matches the outside dimension of the matte.
Use it as backing for the picture.

Now, back to the glass. Remember the glass? Clean it and place it in the frame. Put the matte next, if you have one, with the picture taped on the corners and on the middle of the sides. If you don't have a matte, place the trimmed picture on the glass. Next add the cardboard backing. What you're making is an arty sandwich.

Then pound brads (see page 21) at a very slight downward angle into the frame. This forces the picture flat against the glass. Use a minimum of eight brads, two to a side; more for larger pieces. For hardwood frames, make starter holes with the ice pick, otherwise the brads keep popping out as you try to drive them in. Cover the seams where the cardboard backing and frame meet with masking tape to seal out dirt and moisture.

If you don't want glass over the picture, you should mount it on some sort of a board. Heavy-quality matte or illustration board works fine. Don't use rubber cement to mount the picture if you value it. It's tempting and easy, but it will eventually stain through the front of the picture. There are some glues now on the market that claim to have nonstaining properties, but I don't trust them to withstand the test of time. As far as I know, the best mounter is still photographic mounting tissue, available in various sizes at art and photography supply stores. It's a very thin paper coated on both sides with an adhesive that's activated by heat and sealed down by pressure. Professional photographers have a special heated press, but you can do it with your iron, a strong hand and a desk blotter.

Cut the tissue the same size as the picture to be mounted. If the picture is larger than the tissue, you can piece the tissue together for a fit. The seams won't show. On a table or ironing board with the picture face down, place the tissue on it and lightly touch each corner with the hot iron. This holds the tissue in position. Then turn over the picture with the attached tissue and put it on the mounting board. To be sure it stays where you want it, cover only part of the picture with the blotter to start, holding the other part down with your hand. Iron (no steam here) over the blotter with a hot iron. I've used the "Linen" setting. Be sure that the iron doesn't run over onto the picture itself, and don't stay too long in any one place until you see how it goes.

You don't want to scorch the picture, and you can always go back over it. If you're working with a priceless treasure, first experiment on something akin in weight to get the feel and know-how. Proceed after the mounting to trim and frame as before.

Picture Hanging. To hang a picture you've got to have something to hang it with. This means screw eyes and wire if they're not already on the frame. Start by putting in the two screw eyes to hold the wire. Preferably put them in on the insides of the frame, parallel to the backing if you can. Placed there, they don't show, nor do they keep the picture farther away from the wall than need be.

Always put the screw eyes well above the center of the frame. This keeps the picture from slanting too far forward from the top. Judge how close you get to the top by the size of the picture hanger you will be using. Remember that some of the larger ones are 2″ and 3″ long and they'll show if you go too high.

Make a starter hole with the ice pick and work the screw eyes in first by hand, tightening with pliers if necessary. Take picture wire twice as long as the distance between the screw eyes plus 4″. Thread the wire through both eyes and center like a shoe lace. Then bring each end back through the eye and once around the stem. Bring the ends together in the center and do a Western Union splice (page 64).

Most of this procedure sounds dull and it is. But if any of you have braced a custom-framer lately, you'll soon decide dullness isn't such a bad idea. One interesting little frame I had made cost four times more than what was in it. Ugh!

The hangers cited on page 22 pretty well explain themselves. For very heavy pictures or mirrors consider using a Molly or the plaster nail.

Measure across the top of the frame and divide by two to get the middle. Pull the picture wire with your finger to the maximum stretch of the wire and measure up to the top frame edge.

Hold the picture to the wall where you want it and lightly draw a short line with a pencil on the wall where the top and one side of the frame should go. For heavy jobs it helps greatly if you have the steady hand of a friend.

On the wall, duplicate the measurements you took before on the back of the picture. Measure down from the middle of the top line and across from the side line and X the spot where they meet. Beware! The X is where the hook part of the hanger should end, not where the nail goes in. It's often suggested that you put clear sticky tape over where you're going to nail and it will keep the paint and plaster from cracking when you install the hanger. My experience has been that when you remove the hanger and tape, a piece of wall peels off anyway. Do as you wish. After all is said and hung, if you decide the picture is a little high or a little low, you can usually loosen or tighten the wire to make slight adjustments.

An A.I.D.* will probably flip his wrist or get the vapors over some of the following nuggets regarding picture arrangement. So be it. There are all sorts of rules about what and how you hang on your walls. One old rule I thought was long buried is: Hang pictures at eye level. Whose? I think pictures should relate to stationary objects around them like the wall, a window, a lamp,

a sofa, desk, chest, whatever, not to people. They move. If you have a big, tall table lamp, for instance, don't try to crowd a picture in behind it. That does disservice to both. How about something between the shade and the base—or beside. This brings me to one rule I learned in art school that I heartily subscribe to. Odd numbers of things always look better than even numbers of things. Oh, sure there are the classic arrangements.

* A for-real decorator.

But somehow it always seems more interesting to do

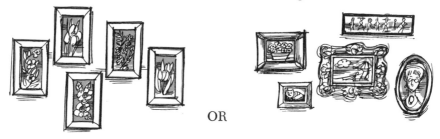

OR

For an "arrangement" of several pieces, some cautious types advise cutting out equal-sized pieces of paper, taping them on the wall and moving them around until they're happy with the look. This works quite well and does save glaring nail holes if you goof. Use masking tape. Unlike the clear tape, it won't take the paint off the wall.

I usually put all the pictures and miscellaneous hangings to be considered on the floor in front of the wall I'm dressing up and arrange them there. You have the color variations, the wall length to judge by, and you have only to worry about the height. When you've decided you like what you've arranged, measure distances between items and mark them down so you don't lose your way as you put the items up. The best place to start is the focal-point picture, because it's the largest or the one you like best. Work the others from there.

Shelves

PUTTING UP. There are two kinds of shelves—ones that are supposed to look good and ones that aren't. The shelves that aren't (or it doesn't matter) are inside cabinets and can be used to relieve overpopulation of staples and supplies. Many places, apartments particularly (starting with those put up in the fifties) go overboard on closets and are chintzy on kitchen cupboards. Other kitchens have a broom closet which can make a better, more efficient cupboard (by installing narrow shelves) for canned goods, cereals and miscellaneous groceries than it is for a mop and broom.

The way to convert a broom closet depends on whether it's metal or wood. If it's metal it is usually free-standing, which means you can pull it out from the wall and get to the sides. Sometimes it will be attached to the wall with a couple of screws. Unscrew and the closet should come free with a little wrenching and screeching.

Saw 1″ x 2″ lumber in lengths equal to the depth of the closet, minus a couple of inches, or to the depth you want the shelves to be. 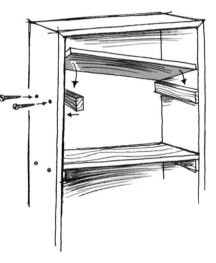 You don't want the shelves right up to the door, as it may not close properly. You will need two pieces of lumber to support each shelf. (These "shelf holders" usually don't show, so you don't have to paint them.) For full-depth shelves, saw ½″ to ¾″ plywood to size; for lesser depths, use 1″ lumber in the width of your choice.

To install shelves, measure equal distances down each side for the number of shelves you want. Drill two holes (see page 3) on each side of the cabinet for each shelf. Take one of the 1″ x 2″ wood lengths, hold it centered over the two holes inside the cupboard, and mark the wood through the holes.

Remove and make starter holes in the wood with a hammer and nail. Put back in position and use a wood screw with a head bigger than the hole and a shank smaller than the hole. Screw the wood tightly in place. Do the same until all the shelf holders are in. Then simply drop the shelves on top of the runners, paint or cover with self-adhesive plastic, and you've got yourself a resting place for easy-to-reach, highly visible supplies.

If the broom closet is wood, you can work from the inside, simply screwing the "shelf holders" into the sides. Watch the length of the screw so you don't go through any exposed sides.

If the broom closet is a cubbyhole with a door set right in the plaster wall, you can use plaster nails to put up the 1" x 2" lengths of wood Use this approach if you want to convert a larger closet for storage. Many overcloseted apartments have a closet somewhere near the kitchen which can be made into a combo food, liquor and cleaning-supplies hiding place. Don't bother to remove the clothes rod. It's usually close under the supplied shelf and won't get in the way of the new shelf below.

You do the side–shelf-holder routine with plaster nails. If the closet is fairly wide, you should put in a supporter in the back to keep the shelf from sagging from the weight of the various and sundry items planned for it. When you're measuring the back, don't forget to figure on the width of side shelf holders.

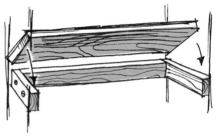

You can partition to leave a verti-

cal area for a stepstool, ladder, rug
shampooer, vacuum or mop.

Saw or have sawed ¾" or 1" plywood to the depth of the shelves
you want and to the height from
the floor to the existing top shelf.
Since you want a *tight* fit, measure
from the front and back for the
distance between the shelf and floor
to be sure. The floor and the shelf
are probably crooked. For this re-
modeling, take out the clothes rod
if you can. If you can't, use the keyhole saw to cut out a hole at the
top of the plywood panel so the pole
can go through. Nail or screw the
side runners on this piece before
you wedge it in. This wedging
operation should take some hammer
work to ensure a tight fit. Many
closet floors are not wood, so you
have to depend on this squeeze
play to hold the plywood wall in
place. This, plus nails down through
the existing shelf into this vertical
piece, will do it. If the floor is wood
you can usually "toe-in" (nail at an
angle through the wood into the
floor) nails and don't have to worry
with such a tight fit. Put up the
other shelf holders on the other wall
of the closet. You may want to do
this before putting up the vertical
board, especially if you're not going
very wide with the shelves. You'll

have more hammering room. Throughout all of this, a spirit level (see page 13) can help keep things on an even keel.

SHOW-OFF SHELVES. The most popular and versatile, and certainly (if you move around a lot) the most practical shelf is the standard-and-bracket variety in either metal or wood. The standard is a raised vertical strip with evenly spaced holes or slots. The bracket locks in to these openings at right angles to form a holder for wood or glass shelves. You can buy different lengths of both standards (you can also have them cut to a specific measure) and brackets to make a variety of arrangements possible. To give you some ideas, here are some of the shelves I've done:

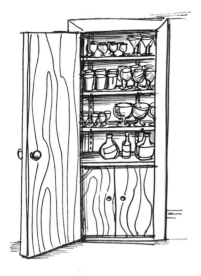

For my money, the standards for these shelves should be put up with either Mollys or lead shields with screws. I had one near-disaster (nothing broke) with the plastic-type fastener—like 1-2-3, all fall down. I know of two other instances where this lighter fastener just couldn't hold the weight of books or hi-fi equipment.

Decide where you want the shelves to be, then start with the top of one standard. Mark the wall through the top screw hole in the standard. Drill a hole in the wall and put in the fastener. (Don't forget Disasters—How to Recoup and Overcome, page 53, if you run into trouble). Then screw the standard tightly enough to the wall so you can move it without its swinging loosely. Use your spirit level to get the standard straight up and down. Hold the standard in place and mark the other screw holes. Loosen the top screw slightly so you can push the standard aside while you install the other fasteners. Return the standard to place, then start and half tighten all screws before finishing up any one.

Measure the same distance down where you want the next standard to go. Mark lightly with a pencil and hold that standard up to the mark. Some standards have a top and bottom, so check that the slots start the same distance from the end. Also check the ceiling line to be sure it's straight. The slots of these standards have to be in line with each other. Do this by laying a yardstick across the top of the two standards (holding the noninstalled on the mark) and putting your spirit level on the yardstick. Mark the top screw hole and do as before.

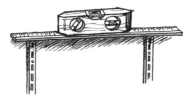

For longer shelves, use at least three standards across, or after a while your books will look like they're in a hammock. Generally, you can figure 30″ to 36″ between standards. Attach the brackets where you think you want them and lay the shelves on them. The great thing about standard/bracket shelves is that you are not confined to one length, width or level. Move them around until you're happy with the arrangement. It helps to put books and bric-a-brac on them to judge distances and design.

For the metal standards and brackets, you can buy pine or birch lumber for shelves and stain or paint them. You can also buy shelves of solid teak and walnut or a veneered version of these woods. The latter is less expensive and the depth is not limited by lumber size. When you work with wood standards and brackets, usually the shelves are part of the package. These are considerably more expensive than the metal version. If you don't like the metal look of the standards, you can paint them to match the wall. Here's where that paint you so cleverly saved comes in handy.

To keep books from falling anywhere along the line, you can buy covered wire book holders that slip on the front of the shelf. If

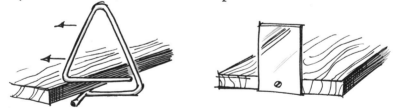

the books will go the whole length of the shelf, you can buy brushed brass rectangles that screw into the ends of the shelves to keep the books in place. When you move you can simply take the shelves, brackets and standards down and with you. Bury the evidence as described on page 79.

Another type of shelf is one that
hangs on the wall with no visible
means of support. The illusion is
easily obtained. Each of the ends
of the shelf has a keyhole-looking
opening on its backside.

Hold the shelf up to the wall
where you want to hang it and
mark the wall at the top of one end.
Measure down on the backside of
the end to just below the top of the
keyhole. This allows for the diameter of the screw. Measure the same
distance from your mark on the
wall. Drill a hole (page 53) and
insert a lead shield and a wide, flat-
headed screw.

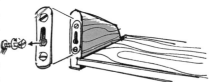

Check the screw with the keyhole
opening before you put it in the
wall to be sure that the diameter of
the screw shank is not too wide to
slip up into the narrower part of the
keyhole and that the head of the
screw is large enough to catch.

Put the screw in almost flush with
the wall, leaving just enough room
to latch on to the keyhole. This
ensures that the shelf is tight to the
wall, not tipped forward. Hook the
end of the shelf onto the screw,
holding the other not-yet-fastened
end. Put the spirit level on the shelf
and when it's level, mark the wall
where the top of that end of the
shelf fits. Take the shelf off and

measure down from the mark where the other screw should be. Drill as before and insert shield there.

If you're off slightly and the screws don't quite match their keyholes, the shelf won't lock in place. Dot the head of one of the screws with light colored paint. When you try the shelf again this will mark where and how much you're missing. Lightly tap the side of the screw to line it up.

Wall Coverings

This term sounds so utilitarian that it denies the tremendous soul lifting these "coverings" can do for a room. The types available are wallpaper, vinyl-coated fabric, self-adhesive plastic sheeting and fabric. The colors and patterns are fabulous and multitudinous. You can convert a cell of a bathroom to an oasis quicker than a missionary can get a Mother Hubbard on a heathen.

Wallpaper. For years the manufacturers offered the dreariest or cutesiest colors and designs. Depending on your age, you may remember when all bathrooms, for instance, *had* to have an aquatic theme. This usually meant water lilies, coral, seaweed, water-addicted birds (for some reason ducks never much made it, but swans and cranes were big) and fish. It's little wonder the painted wall won out. At least over paint you could put up your own meaningful bad stuff rather than some character's idea of tallyho, the fox or a hammered-out texture.

Today's paper is wondrously changed. Besides having marvelous designs, almost all are coated to give them at the least a wipe-offable surface and one that makes the paper sturdy enough so that you don't stick your thumb through it when you put it up.

Although some wallpapers now claim a "removable" quality, most of them are somewhat messy. If you rent, try to "sell" the next tenant on your taste, or be prepared to get some complaints from the landlord. There is a "removing" liquid which you dilute with water and apply with a wide brush, let soak and then scrape off the paper with a putty knife. It works better than just plain water, but it still takes time and more than the promised "one application does it" if there's more than one layer of paper. Don't even think of renting a steamer. Lose part of your security deposit if need be. It's worth it if you've enjoyed your walls.

Vinyl-coated Fabric. This, too, is miles ahead of the old oil-cloth school. In many ways, this is what you should use as your first try at hanging. It stands up under early, clumsy handling—much pushing and pulling to adjust and fit. Paste and grubby fingerprints wipe right off. It's truly scrubbable and best of all, as mentioned on page 79, for renters, it will pull down with no difficulty. Start at one corner and pull diagonally. Off she comes.

Self-adhesive Plastic Sheeting. This is the same great stuff you use to line cupboards and drawers. The manufacturers think it's great for walls, too. I don't. It's maddening to handle in longer lengths. I once did one kitchen wall, floor to ceiling, in a Scotchplaid pattern. Never again in lengths like those in any pattern! It sticks before you want it to, and if you pull it up for a better match or to get rid of large bubbles, it stretches. My advice is to forget it unless you only have a small area where you can handle it much like the lining operation.

Fabric. If you choose to do a wall, a folding screen or window shades in oriental silk, you're on your own. I'm really a cotton or burlap type. If the material you use will shrink, wash and dry it first. Buy cellulose paste at a hardware or wall-covering store.

Here we go again with the bathtub. Mix the paste there. This gives you plenty of elbowroom to immerse the lengths of fabric. Measure and cut the fabric, allowing a couple of inches leeway. Submerge the strip in the paste and proceed as you would for the other past-needing wall coverings (page 169). Interestingly enough, when the paste dries it acts as a dirt protector on the fabric surface.

Self-adhesive fabrics are available but they're murderously expensive.

❈   ❈   ❈

(To simplify things from now on, I'll use the term "paper" unless there's an exception you need to know about.

❈   ❈   ❈

Applicators and Miscellaneous Materials. All these items are quite inexpensive and you may already have some of them on hand.

PASTE BRUSH is a flat, sisal-like brush about 10″ to 12″ wide. You use it to swab the paste on the back of nonprepasted paper.

WALL BRUSH is also a wide flat brush without a handle. It's used to smooth down the paper after it's placed on the wall. Used at right angles, it will tuck and fit paper along edges and into corners.

BUCKET. Either use a household pail or buy a big size of the disposable paper one. The bucket must be wide enough at the top to take the paste brush.

PAPER CUTTER. Forget this for the money you want to spend. There's no such thing, cheap, that will hold a cutting edge, even through a small job. Use a razor-blade knife or scissors instead.

PASTE used to be a bore to mix to get the lumps out of it. It still is, unless you spend a little more and buy a "new, improved" version. It's worth every extra cent. The paste mixes much more easily, adheres better and usually has an anti-mildew agent in it.

SEAM ROLLER is a small (usually wooden) wide wheel that you run along the paper edges and seams to press them down firmly. If you don't want to bother, a combination of pounding with the wall brush and running the flat of your thumbnail along the seam works quite well. However, for flocked paper, a roller should not be used because it flattens the fuzz.

SIZING is basically a gluey mix you apply to the wall before papering, mostly on new plaster or glossy paint for better adhesion. It's particularly good with heavier-bodied coverings whose surface strength tends to pull them away from the wall.

SPONGE. Dampen with clean water to wipe off excess, oozy paste at the seams and on the paper itself after you have put it up.

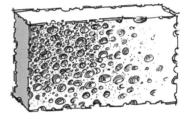

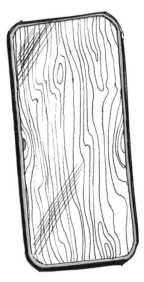

BED BOARD. Don't order this until you fall off a ladder. But if you already have fallen or have one, a bed board makes an extremely good pasting board. Place it on a bed or across the dining table. Cover the board with newspapers to absorb slopped-over paste. If you don't have a bed board or a large table, newspapers on the floor in copious amounts act admirably. Spread the newspapers to the length, and more, of the longest piece of paper you'll be hanging, and in overlapping layers. Then, when you have excess paste on one layer, you can roll it up and throw away. This keeps a good deal of paste off the surface of the wallpaper.

Theoretically, you won't need all these supplies if you buy a *prepasted* type of wall covering. But don't pass up a nonprepasted pattern you love just because prepasted sounds so easy. Sometimes it isn't. As you must already have discovered, things are seldom what they seem.

For prepasted paper you're supposed to use an E-Z Water Box which the manufacturer recommends. Just fill the box with water, put the box under your working area, reverse-roll the strip of paper, soak for a minute or so and simply haul the paper up, up and away into place. Got it?

The prepasted paper I wanted was wider than any water box on the scene, so I used the bathtub. This is fine when you're doing a bathroom (I was), but for other rooms with paper from the same manufacturer, a friend and I used the bathtub and then had to run through other rooms with the paper streaming gluey water. Painter's drop cloths and newspaper strewn along the trail helped, but it was sloppy going.

Also, when the paper is submerged, air bubbles form within

the roll and keep the water from reaching all the paste areas. Naturally, unless you keep poking at the paper, box or no, you don't discover this until you unroll the paper. Recoup madly with a sopping sponge.

HOW TO ORDER YOUR WALL COVERING. Measure the length and the height of the walls you're going to cover, also any large openings. Take these measurements with you to the store. Remember that the width of the paper and whether there is a "match" problem pretty much determine how much paper you should order above what your measurements indicate. If you have a reasonably good head for figures, you yourself can etsimate the amount of paper needed by working with the width and roll length printed on the back of the sample paper in the book.

Paper usually comes in double rolls. This is an advantage if you're using a lot of paper that requires matching. It's an expensive penalty if you're doing a small area. Look through the remnants and returns—you may find a bargain.

If you choose a paper that has a "drop match" pattern you will have a "loss" of varying inches depending on the size of the pattern. I've had it vary from somewhere around 8″ on one pattern to 18″ on another. To match, you allow extra paper to fill the gap. This is as good a time as any to suggest stripes. They're glorious ceiling raisers and accents with no match problem at all, just a side-by-side progression right down the wall.

HOW TO HANG WALLPAPER. Before you start, check the walls. For never-before-covered walls, consider washing (see page 138) or sizing (see page 167). For previously covered walls, watch out for loose edges. Either paste down or scrape off. If the paper you've picked doesn't have a "drop match," you probably can go ahead and cut the full-length strips, allowing about 3″ to

4″ extra. You'll cut it off later. That's what the experts say, but I've always been timid about doing this. Besides, I really don't understand how they can say that. Except for stripes, almost every paper has a match of some sort, "drop" or not. I usually cut one strip and put it up, and then hold up the next strip-to-be while still on the roll to see where and how it falls. Dull of me, maybe, but I find it less nerve-racking.

Definitely follow this routine for the "drop match" so you can determine how much to chop or leave to ensure a match. If you're going to paper all the way around a room, start in a corner behind the door. Chances are you'll be slightly off when you end up. It won't show so much.

To get off to a straight start, measure from the corner out the width of the paper at three or four places down the wall. Since most corners are crooked, you can hang a line from the top and let gravity judge the straightness of the wall for you. Take a string the height of the wall and tie a spoon on one end. Tape or tack the string on your mark near the ceiling. Make the string short enough to clear the baseboard and to hang free. Check your marks against the string line and adjust accordingly. Draw a line, bearing in mind that the string is right regardless of how much off it may look.

Put paste on the back of the first strip of paper, starting at the top. Don't be skimpy with the paste, especially along the edges. If the strip is longer than the pasting area you're working on, paste a section, fold it over, paste to paste, and move the strip up off the newspaper and continue pasting. This will get some paste on the surface of the wallpaper but you can sponge it off later. Usually, however, I don't fold over the top because it's one thing less to unfurl when you get to the wall. I do fold over, paste to paste, a good portion of the bottom after the whole strip is pasted. It pulls apart easily. For short pieces this isn't necessary, but for longer strips it makes the paper much easier to carry and handle.

Pick up the paper gingerly by the top corners. Put the paper to the ceiling, allowing an inch or so to go above it. If you're not papering the entire room, start the paper flush with the corner. If you are doing the whole room, start the paper about 1″ around the corner. This may vary depending on what you've learned from your string hanging. You can fill in a patch if you have to after you've finished the main part. When you have the paper lined up, take the paper brush and smooth the paper down to where it's folded under. Use the bristle ends to pound the paper into the corner. Don't worry if the paper doesn't reach your drawn line as long as you are parallel to it. The paper will want to peel off at the top so hold it in place with the brush while you unfold the bottom part of the paper. The weight of the paper will make it drop. Continue to smooth down with the brush. If air bubbles develop (and they will), try to smooth toward the edge to get them out. If they persist or you're off line, pull the paper back up or down a bit, reseat it on the wall and smooth. Because of the plastic coatings on many papers and fabrics, small bubbles will not disappear despite your most dedicated brushing.

Don't brush the paper to death. This type of "bubble" will flatten out as the paper dries on the wall. It'll take some hours, so don't stew. Trim any excess paper at the top and bottom as you go along. Get your trim line by running closed scissors' blades along the ceiling and baseboard. If the line is irregular and lumpy from old paint and plaster, it's better to pull back the paper and cut it straight with scissors. The bumps tend to send a razor blade off in directions not altogether pleasing. If the line is smooth, by all means use the razor-blade knife.

Get your match for the second strip, if it is a match pattern, and repeat the routine. The only difference here is the "butting" of new paper against that on the wall. "Butting" simply means to get so close that they touch. Use the wall brush and the heel of your hand to "move" the paper in. Run the seam roller or your thumbnail down the hairline. Lightly wipe off any oozed paste or gooey finger and hand prints. If you've skimped or skipped on paste and an edge doesn't want to stay down, don't try to use the brush. It's too big. Take a piece of the paper you've trimmed off, fold it pattern to pattern to expose the pasted side. This gives you a double-sided paste surface which you slip under the dry spot. Usually there's enough paste to do the job. If not, dip it in the paste and use.

When you come to an opening, be it a door, window, fireplace, whatever, measure from your last strip (or from the corner of the wall if the opening is near). If more paper will be over the opening than on the wall, cut the paper before you put it up, allowing excess for crookedness. Check by measuring top and bottom and cut accordingly. Save the "holes" for piecing. If they're already pasted, fold the pasted surfaces together. This will keep them wet enough to use later on—not the next day, understand, but in three or four hours, depending on humidity or lack of it. If finishing the job has to wait overnight or for several hours, put foil or plastic covering over the paste bucket. When you start again and the paste has become too thick, add some water and stir.

The first strip is the hardest so don't lose heart. Dexterity comes with practice. Also be of good cheer if a bubble stays or the match isn't absolute. You are examining every flaw. It'll never show on a galloping horse.

Some friends of mine did a whole kitchen totally unaware that they were dealing with a "drop match" pattern. They just lined up all the Major Grey's Chutney jars of the pattern on the ceiling line. Truncated philodendron vines, Liver Pa instead of Liver Paté and halved pepper grinders went undiscovered for some months. The denouement came when another friend and I were using the leftovers to do a small wall in her apartment kitchen. We kept runnning out of the Liver Paté match. Chutney was in short supply, too. We called to see if there were any more scraps and the truth was revealed. We cheated by cutting out philodendron leaves and pasted them on top of the more obvious dead ends. Nobody ever noticed that either. So relax!

Okay, You've Done It!!!

If you're still beleaguered by a flickery light, a boring wall or various unhung goodies, look, dear Brutus, not to the stars. You honestly can do everything that's described in this book and probably much, much more. One aside: Don't do anything you're truly afraid to do—I don't mean timid or unconfident—I mean really afraid. A shaky surgeon is a lousy choice for an appendectomy. I can only repeat the most important ingredients for success of any project:

1. Believe you can do it. Remember some of the all-thumbs types who have done work for you in the past. Don't dwell on the thought if you're married to one. Realize the truth. You really can do it.
2. Be prepared for things to go wrong or at least differently from what you expect or others promise. Don't panic. There's always some way out of the maze.
3. Be sensible about what you do try. If you're dead tired—stop! If you've had a bad day—don't start.
4. Get a friend to lend a hand. You can always do a home and home series. Almost any project is more fun and easier with help unless you're inexplicably blessed with an unhandy friend. If so, let her come over and cook.
5. Don't expect perfection. You don't get it even when you pay and you won't get it when you do it, either. But you'll be close enough to afford to be a bit smug.

The rewards are multifaceted. There's money-saving, of course, and time, convenience, comfort, beauty and plain self-satisfaction. Lots of funny things will happen to you, too, as news of your prowess spreads. One of my favorite stories is about going to a friend's apartment to put up standards and brackets for shelves. I decided it was stupid to drag along a bulky purse as well as the heavy toolbox. I simply put my make-up case, wallet and keys in the top tray of the toolbox. The sweet logic of this thought departed fast when I saw the "what kind of nut is this?" look on the cabby's face when I opened my "purse" to pay him. In cases like this, don't explain. Carry it off the best you can and retreat before they come after you with a net.

Index

About the Author

BARBARA CURRY's early do-it-yourself days were in Ohio. Despite some failures, like building an orange-crate boat (it promptly sank —she didn't seal between the slats) and painting a wagon red directly below her mother's wash (a spanking), she survived to win local library reading contests (nobody else entered). College included projects like building a balcony for a chorus of Juliets (it scares her to think of it now) and a B.A. in art and psychology.

After slaving as a company photographer/artist (her bonus was $20 and an apple), Barbara went to New York and became a writer for leading advertising agencies. She credits keeping her sanity in that world to putting up bookshelves. With a co-op apartment in New York City and a house in New Jersey to keep in practice, Barbara spends any free time she has on free-lance writing and answering her friends' calls for HELP!